Acclaim for Samantha Irby's

meaty

An Emily Books Book Club Selection

A *Publishers Weekly* Big Indie Books of Fall

A *Cosmopolitan* Best 22 Books of the Year for Women, by Women

"Samantha Irby is as bad as she wants to be." —*Chicago Tribune*

"Raunchy, funny, and vivid. . . . Those faint of heart beware. . . .
Strap in and get ready for a roller-coaster ride to remember."
—*Kirkus Reviews*

"Amazingly crass, defiant, witty, terrifying, and wondrous. . . .
[Irby] cuts the bawdy, wickedly funny pieces with some truly
poignant palate cleansers. . . . Irby's voice is raw, gripping,
and . . . delicious." —*Booklist*

"Her candor in style and subject matter—mostly sex, dating,
and the general lousiness of men—has earned Samantha Irby
a cult following. . . . Honesty mixed with self-deprecating
humor is what propels the reader." —*Time Out Chicago*

Samantha Irby

meaty

Samantha Irby is the author of the *New York Times* bestseller *We Are Never Meeting in Real Life.* and writes a blog called *bitches gotta eat.*

www.bitchesgottaeat.com

meaty

meaty

ESSAYS

samantha irby

VINTAGE BOOKS
A Division of Penguin Random House LLC
New York

A VINTAGE ORIGINAL, APRIL 2018

Copyright © 2013, 2018 by Samantha Irby

All rights reserved. Published in the United States by Vintage Books,
a division of Penguin Random House LLC, New York, and distributed in
Canada by Random House of Canada, a division of Penguin Random
House Canada Limited, Toronto. Originally published, in different form,
by Curbside Splendor Publishing Inc., Chicago, Illinois, in 2013.

Vintage and colophon are registered trademarks of
Penguin Random House LLC.

"My Mother, My Daughter" previously appeared on *The Rumpus*.

Some names and identifying details have been changed
to protect the privacy of individuals.

The Cataloging-in-Publication data is available from the
Library of Congress.

Vintage Books Trade Paperback ISBN: 978-0-525-43616-4
eBook ISBN: 978-0-525-43617-1

Book design by Anna B. Knighton

www.vintagebooks.com

Printed in the United States of America
10 9 8 7 6 5 4 3 2 1

This book is dedicated to that kid Maurice in my US history class junior year who called me a fucking idiot.

LOL, BRUH.

Dudes, I'm not a pig.

I didn't just slap an adorable new cover on the same piece of garbage you bought a few years ago to try to trick you out of couch-cushion money you could have otherwise been spending on beer. This turd has actually been polished! I wrote some new stuff, and the old stuff has been lovingly edited by a team of fancy people in New York.

Besides, when I die prematurely of secondhand embarrassment because some jerk decided to propose to his girlfriend in the same restaurant I'm just trying to eat dinner in, the old edition will be a collector's item!

Samantha Irby
December 2017

CONTENTS

brunch

· · · · · · · · · · · · · · · · ·

an instagram frittata

Back in the olden days when everyone was shouting into Nokia flip phones and scratched-up Razrs and you didn't have to worry about whether your breakfast would look cute in someone's newsfeed, when people would come over to my crib (i.e., wake up in my apartment to find themselves disappointed by my lack of a coffeemaker or anything resembling a wholesome breakfast food), I would do that thing where I throw a bunch of leftover garbage into however many eggs I could salvage from the dented carton of them chilling in the back of the fridge and bake it in a superhot oven until it sort of resembled a brown egg flatbread, then emerge from the kitchen like "Ta-da! I am a capable adult-type human!"

Ingredients

1 potato

1 red pepper, cored and seeded, sliced into thin strips

1 onion, sliced not diced, because it looks more elegant
   that way

6–8 eggs

sea salt and pepper

some bagged spinach or kale, unless you're the kind of
   asshole who has that shit growing outside your well-
   tended home

oil or butter, it doesn't matter

maybe some bacon if you want, or ham could be good
   too!

2 teaspoons rosemary, if you like that kind of thing

1 cup of whatever grated cheese you have left over from
   your last nacho day

I am not an egg person. Egg people enjoy thick, slimy yolks
splooging over their tongues as they take a bite of their fried-
egg sandwiches; they like rivulets of yellow slime cascading from
under their hamburger buns; they squeal with delight as a pud-
dle of neon goo oozes from their freshly poached eggs to settle
wetly around the edge of their avocado toasts. But eggs are so
cheap, and people always buy them, and making a frittata is way
better than saying "Sunny-side-up eggs make me want to die"
when they are your only option for food.

1. Crack the eggs into a bowl and beat them with a whisk.
   If owning a whisk is the kind of thing that is too fancy
   for you, throw this book in the trash.

2. Add to the eggs a couple of pinches of salt and a grind or two of pepper. I never measure, because am I really supposed to grind the peppermill over a teaspoon and see how much I can catch? I'm not doing that! Just shake your sea salt container a few times and grind the pepper three or four times so that you can see black specks floating around after you stir it again to mix it all up.

3. Suddenly remember that you forgot the *actual* first steps, which are: wash and slice your potato into thin disks (use a mandoline and watch your fingers); wash, core, and seed your red pepper, slicing into skinny strips; cut your onion, but not into chunks, because chunks are weird feeling in eggs. Okay, here's how I do it: I cut off both the top and the bottom of the onion so that I have a flat surface to balance them on, then I take a sharp paring knife and cut from top to bottom while turning the onion an eighth of an inch at a time, until it all falls apart and looks like rainbows scattered across the cutting board.

Now is about the time I feel like I've accomplished a lot. So I usually take a break, which often involves admiring my beautiful pile of uniformly cut vegetables while drinking coffee and wondering whether this will actually be worth it in the end.

4. I always forget until it's too late that lettuce should probably be cleaned, so now is a good time to find whatever moldering kale or spinach is hanging out at the bottom

of your crisper drawer and dump it into a bowl that is 1 cup distilled white vinegar to 3 cups cold water and soak it for 2 minutes, then rinse it in a colander and maybe shake it a little to get some of the water out. I know it feels like a lot of work—and I'm not going to lie, I've probably eaten forty-seven *E. coli* salads since last Tuesday—but now that I'm thinking about it, if you gotta eat greens, at least maybe try not to die from them.

5. Set your responsibly washed old salad aside and heat up some oil or butter in a deep cast-iron pan and preheat your oven to 400 degrees Fahrenheit (cue Juvenile's "400 Degreez"). Cook the potatoes first, for five minutes, over medium heat, moving them around a little bit so they don't stick or burn. Then add the onions and peppers and cook for another five minutes, moving everything around but not so rough that you turn it into gross mush. At this point you could add some crumbled cooked bacon, but that adds a series of extra steps that I'm not gonna do while hungover on a Sunday. So it's a no from me, dog. But I might chop some deli ham and toss it in there if I have it, but again, probably not. Anyway, if you're putting meat in this, chop it up and throw it in now. Also, at some point during this process, sprinkle salt and pepper on it.

6. Add the rosemary and the shredded cheese dregs to your beaten eggs (remember them?!) and stir. Then flatten out the vegetables in the hot pan as best you can and pour the egg mixture over it. Shake off your ripped-up

chard or kale or spinach and kinda just gently press it into everything; don't add so much that it doesn't mix in, eyeball the right amount. Scroll through your Insta feed and look at pretty brunch spreads. No one wants a glorified egg pizza with a bunch of dried-up grass sitting on top of it.

7. Bake it for twenty minutes, give or take, until it's set. Keep an eye on it starting around the fifteen-minute mark. I like mine a little brown on top, because jiggly eggs in my mouth make me want to cry, but you can eat yours however you want.

I'm not an expert on how to pose food to ensure maximum jealousy from people you went to high school with twenty years ago, but here is what I'd try:

1. Use a trivet so you can set the pan on your nicest table surface without fear of ruining it. Oh, you eat on TV trays but you have a rustic chest of drawers next to your bed? You better run that skillet upstairs, girl!

2. So people know that you actually made it with your own hands, scatter some eggshells and salmonella around the countertops so potential dates know that you don't go to the farmers' market just to take pictures of purple carrots. (I go to the farmers' market just to take pictures of purple carrots.)

3. Buy one nice plate. It doesn't even have to be a fancy plate; just get something that looks good through the

lens of a dying iPhone. SpaghettiOs look like high art in a gleaming Crate and Barrel square cereal bowl.

4. Nice napkins can serve the dual purpose of making you feel like a capable adult and also making pictures of your revolting home food look more palatable. Plus they're pretty cheap, and if you buy one of each color/style, no one has to know that you don't have the whole set unless they swing by demanding to look at your linen cabinet, but even then you can just brush them off like, "Who cares about matching?" and their eyes will widen in awe at how breezy and bohemian you are when really you just wanted a prop for some gluten-free brownies.

I have this dream of one day working up the courage to post pictures of the remnants of food that I've already maxed: miserable-looking hot dog butts, dried soup ring crusts on a tower of stacked bowls, gnawed-on breadsticks, the last two pieces of cereal floating in some rancid milk skin. Until then, I guess I'll just be over here artfully setting my fork at a ninety-degree angle next to this perfect cassoulet I made for the express purpose of hopefully impressing that guy who once laughed at me for pronouncing the *t*.

at thirty

Today, February 13, 2010, is my birthday. I am excited because
I am thirty years old and I don't have a man in my life. I haven't
had any children. I haven't finished college. I don't have any
major accomplishments of note. I don't own any property. I
have a "job" and not a "career." I am incapable of going grocery
shopping. (In my refrigerator: Campari, club soda, orange juice,
and High Life.) I haven't paid my electric bill in the last three
months. I have a broken foot that won't heal. I'm not that smart.
I have squamous metaplasia in my ileum. I can't see shit. The
radiator in my bathroom is broken, but I haven't called my landlord because I need to take the garbage out first (and pick up all
the dirty panties piled next to the toilet). I still don't know how
to work my fucking phone.

I can't make pancakes. I busted my laptop and can't afford

a new one right now. My novel is finished but unedited and unpublished because I busted my laptop and can't afford a new one right now. I don't have cable. The pants I'm wearing right this second have a hole in le snatch. My stomach hurts ALL THE FUCKING TIME, and these drugs are making me too sick to properly function. I'm trying to be a vegetarian now, but I keep sneaking chicken. I can't hear, either. Sometimes I'm just not that nice. I laugh at a lot of stupid shit. I have to wear a diaper sometimes at night when my Crohn's is acting like a bitch. I haven't voted since 2001. My hair is totally crazy. I am into way too much age-inappropriate music. It is impossible for me to listen to my voice mails. I snore. I can't do Sudoku. My nails are too long for my liking right now. I have an attitude. My neck hurts. I have weird patches of hair in unexpected places. I have a horrible sweet tooth.

I should fucking work out. I can't work out because my Achilles and broken foot are ruined. I am irritated 99.8 percent of the time. I *hate* everything. I *loathe* everyone. I sleep in a full-size bed. I don't know how to fucking alphabetize hyphenated last names. I am constantly seething in jealous rage. I talk a lot of shit. I fight to the death. The smell of Christmas trees makes me sick. I can't stay awake in a movie theater. I am a cat person (sad). I'm ridiculously tormented and moody. I can't have multiple orgasms. I would eat Toaster Strudel every day if I could. Dudes don't promptly return my phone calls. I can't stand Alicia Keys. I have vomited on the train three times in the last eight months, and I fell asleep in a bar two weeks ago.

I need a therapist, and I need a nutritionist. I need someone to style my outfits. I need a tall person to come over and change my light bulbs. I need a cook, and I need a maid. I need to go to the dentist and the gynecologist. I need to pay the podiatrist.

I need to look into retaining an acupuncturist. I need to save up to go to a hypnotist. I need a financial adviser. I need a tax attorney. I need a car so I can go to more shit. I need a person to dig said car out of the snow in the winter and find me a parking space every night within ten blocks of my goddamned apartment because I have to live in Rogers Park where the rent is cheap and I can still get away with waking up forty minutes before I need to have my ass at work.

I need more people to describe me as "the funniest person they know." I need some fucking PARENTS. And maybe even some godparents. I need a brand-new MacBook Pro with endless gigs of RAM. I need a lint roller that actually works, *or* I need a hairless fucking cat. I need Helen to stop sneezing on my clothes in unsuspecting places only for me to discover a dried glob of snot halfway through the day. I need some more friends. I need a fucking loan. I need braces. I need a massage. I need a pedicure. I need $465 to give to Mel so he will stop calling me *every single day.*

I need some hot dudes around who want to get half naked with me (I like to remain semi-clothed during sex). I need some ugly dudes around to make me feel good about myself. I need some smart dudes around to help me cheat the government and take over the planet. I need some muscly dudes around to carry my shit for me. I need some angry dudes around to beat bitches up when they fuck with me. I need some literate dudes around to do my homework. I need some girly dudes around to keep my eyebrow game on point. I need some salty dudes around to talk shit and giggle with me, and I need some sweet dudes around to keep me from killing ALL THE OTHER TYPES OF DUDES.

I need to find a pharmacist who will exchange medication for blow jobs. I need to have the ability to kill someone with a look. I need to get a bike. I need a Comcast hookup. I need some manners. I need patience. I need a more effective approach to homework. I need a bottle of Maalox. I need a couple of cocktails. I need an eye exam. I need a new gastrointestinal tract. I need to meet Quentin Tarantino. I need for someone to fall desperately in love with me. I also might need a sedative.

I want a piano, because I have played since I was four and it just doesn't feel the same on the keyboard I keep tucked away in the closet. I want to go swimming. I want to eat pizza without puking. I want a pet lion. I want a magic wand. I want to be able to murder in cold blood and not go to jail. I want a flat-screen television. I want a couch on which to sit and gaze at that flat-screen television. I want to learn how to dance for real. I want to do a one-woman show. I want to speak Italian. I want some comfortable shoes. I want five hundred bitches to read my blog every day. I want to learn how to sew so I can try out for *Project Runway*. I want a harem of Asian-looking black dudes or black-looking Asian dudes. I want medical marijuana for this raggedy belly (but only if it won't give me the munchies, because I can't eat *shit* anymore). I want to ride a camel to the club and valet that shit. I want ten tubes of M·A·C's Spring Bean Lustreglass. I want cuter stores in my neighborhood. I want the new Peaches record. I want to see Muse in concert.

I want to get over all my old manfriends alfuckingready. That said, I want dudes to DROP DEAD the second they hurt my tender little feelings. I want more time to read. I want people to stop leaving me Facebook presents. I want some mixtapes from dudes who have hot crushes on me. I want the keys to the kingdom. I want some Fannie May Eggnog Creams. I want a Dilaudid drip next to my bed. I want a leopard Snuggie. I want Jeff

Buckley to rise from the dead. I want to get more of my drinks paid for. I want to live with Nina in San Diego and eat hot carrots and rolled tacos every day. I want fresh flowers delivered to me every day. I want to sleep eighteen hours a day and dance to La Roux for the rest of it. I WANT A WINNING LOTTERY TICKET.

awkward first date

Oh, hi. This restaurant you picked intimidates me. I am not wearing the right footwear for a place this goddamned fancy, and I am probably too poor to eat here in real life, so I am really hoping that you are a gentleman and that this $15 pasta is on you.

Name: Samantha McKiver Irby

Nickname: Everyone has been calling me "Irby" for the last couple of years and at first it was totally fucking weird, but I guess I'm pretty used to it now. My close friends and I call each other "bud." Admitting that to the public makes me feel like we're dumb. Lots of people call me Sam. As a matter of fact, whenever someone says "Samantha," I'm always like, "Oh noes, what did I do wrong?!"

My parents were: Grace Irby, a licensed practical nurse, and Samuel Irby, a professional alcoholic.

You were named after: My middle name, pronounced *Mick-eever*, is my maternal grandmother's maiden name. And the Samuel/Samantha thing, if that didn't click for you a second ago.

The household you grew up in: Changed a lot, and often.

The last time you cried: I'm always fucking crying. It's pathetic. Most recently, I watched Jimmy Fallon and Mariah Carey sing "All I Want for Christmas Is You" with the Roots and a bunch of schoolkids on the Internet and I totally cried. I cried while watching fake Christmas cheer on fucking YouTube. I'm hopeless.

Do you like your handwriting? Yes, it's pretty goddamned amazing. And at the risk of sounding like a stupid asshole, as a kid it was really important to me to have artsy handwriting, so I practiced it and imitated the handwriting of popular girls in my class. To this day I make my *S*'s the way Anna made hers. It's artsy, my handwriting. Ugh. It's so gross even saying that.

Would you kiss the last person you kissed again? Oh God. This is sad. This is so sad because yes, yes I absolutely fucking would. It was Fred, maybe six months ago? And if I'm being totally honest, I'm not quite sure what happened there and why it ended so abruptly, and I am still not over it. Life is hard.

What were you doing three hours ago? Watching concurrent seasons of *The Hills* on Netflix streaming because, in my heart,

I really believe I am a twenty-one-year-old white girl from Southern California. But I was also eating rib tips, which decidedly proves that I most certainly am not.

If you were another person, would you be friends with you? I don't know, man. I guess it depends on the kind of friend you are looking for. If you need the kind of friends who have enough disposable income to help fix your transmission when it blows, or can take off work to spend the day with your sick kid, that might not always be me. But I'm funny and I like to talk shit, and who wouldn't want to be friends with that?

Do you use sarcasm a lot? Not at all. Absolutely never. (I'm being sarcastic.)

Do you still have your tonsils? Yes. And my wisdom teeth. It's like I failed adolescence.

Would you ever bungee jump? That is not for black people. Or fat people. So no.

Have you had sex today? Um. I haven't had sex in 153 days. I've watched a lot of television, though. Ask me about something I actually know about. Ask me about *that* shit.

What is your favorite cereal? Is Triscuit a cereal? What's that one with the corn on one side and the wheat on the other? Not Chex, the other one. Look at me, pretending to be an adult. I'MA STOP LYING NOW: Cinnamon Toast Crunch in a salad bowl, zoned out in front of some cartoons.

Do you untie your shoes before you take them off? Nope. I am too old and tired to wear shoes with complicated laces. I wear Birkenstocks and shit. And, as a matter of fact, I was just on Zappos looking at Velcro New Balance sneakers. I should stop wondering why I'm single.

What is your favorite ice cream? This is like asking me to choose between my imaginary children. But if I'm being forced to Sophie's choice this shit, I choose Ben and Jerry's Pistachio Pistachio.

What is the first thing you notice about people? Their clothes and their bearing. I like stylish people with a presence.

What is your least favorite thing about yourself? My jowls, especially when photographed from certain angles.

Who do you miss the most? I miss the idea of my mother a great deal. My parents have been dead for fifteen years, and since I never got to know them as real adult humans I'm not sure whether I'd like them. Like, what if the reanimated corpse of my mother is a huge bitch? And I used the last of my genie wishes to bring her back to life?! To be safe, I should stick with someone I know I get along with. Or, at least, someone I used to. I miss my old friend Jenny. Relationships end and motherfuckers evolve, and that's cool, but sometimes shit will happen that only she could appreciate, and I miss being able to call her and tell her about dumb shit on television.

What are you listening to right now? Spotify playlist I made specifically for writing shit. A sampling of jams:

"Again (Scratch 22 Remix)" Electric Wire Hustle
"Three Months" Local Natives
"Cola" Toro y Moi
"The Day That Never Comes" Metallica
"Dead Things" Emiliana Torrini
"Fljótavík" Sigur Rós
"Sunday Morning" Ani DiFranco
"Waiting Underground" Patti Smith
"Cosmic Love" Florence and the Machine

What are your favorite smells? C.O. Bigelow's balsam and frankincense candles. Kush-scented oil from the African store down the street from my crib. Kiehl's coriander liquid soap. Jo Malone's French lime blossom.

Who was the last person you talked to on the phone? Caitlin, on speakerphone, while simultaneously pooping and brushing my teeth because I was late for brunch at Au Cheval. For some reason those details seem necessary.

Mountain hideaway or beach house? Beach house. But only because: (1) the idea of my log cabin sliding down the face of a fucking mountain is absolutely terrifying, and (2) the band.

Favorite sport to watch? Football. Big asses + tight, shiny pants = yes, please.

Favorite food? Brunch and tacos.

The last movie you watched? *Side Effects*. In the theater, with popcorn and a Coke. I love me some Soderbergh.

What color shirt are you wearing? I am wearing a black jumpsuit that I often wear as pajamas and as real clothes, because I am creeping ever closer to the glorious day my inside clothes and my outside clothes are the same fucking thing.

Summer or winter? Fall. Sweaters and boots without the slush. Perfect.

Hugs or kisses? Hugs. Sometimes I don't do a thorough job brushing my teeth.

Computer or television? I couldn't possibly choose. And now that I have Hulu and Netflix streaming and a motherfucking iPhone I don't have to.

What book are you reading now?
> *How to Be a Woman* by Caitlin Moran
> *The Fault in Our Stars* by John Green
> *The Round House* by Louise Erdrich

I have a Kindle, which makes it nearly impossible to commit to one book. Also, there's a *BUST* magazine that has been sitting in my bathroom for two weeks that somehow I still have not finished; definitely deserves an honorable mention.

Favorite sound? The humidifier, turned all the way up.

Do you own a pair of skinny jeans? Yes, but after I saw a picture of myself in the newspaper wearing them last summer I am never wearing those assholes in public ever again.

Have you ever ridden in an ambulance? I had a nervous breakdown in college when I was at Northern Illinois University, and my

RA called an ambulance to come and take me to the crazy ward at the local hospital. A really nice police officer sat with me the entire time and eventually drove me back to my dorm once they determined I wasn't going to slit my wrists with a protractor, or something else sharp and collegiate. I wrote that officer a thank-you note that basically read, "You were cool. I'm pretty sure I'm not crazy." Jesus.

Do you play any musical instruments? Nerd alert: I play the piano, the flute, the clarinet, and the saxophone. Some better than others, none well enough to start that disco-reggae band I've been dreaming about.

Are you afraid of the dark? Oh, you think darkness is your ally, but you merely adopted the dark; I was born in it, molded by it. I didn't see the light until I was already a man, and by then it was nothing to me but BLINDING! Just kidding. The answer is no.

If you could wish for one thing, anything you ever wanted, what would it be? An army of weaponized bees.

i want to write your mom's match.com profile

In the fifth grade I was invited to a party. A party at which there was maybe going to be some kissing, at least according to the rumor mill. The party was to be held at Reggie's house, in a large Victorian not far from our elementary school. I'm not quite sure how I even wrangled an invitation, since I knew that no one in attendance would want to kiss me. But I was funny, and likable enough. Or maybe one of the conditions of having people over was that he couldn't leave anyone off the invite list. Thank God for that fucking rule. I shudder to think what my construction paper mailbox would have looked like every adolescent Valentine's Day without it.

My mom had a thing about manners, and she insisted that I both dress up and "take something" to a gathering that was essentially going to be a bunch of shrieking fifth graders wound up on orange pop and pizza shouting in one another's faces. She made me wear what I had worn on picture day the year before, a red dress with a delicate floral print and puffy, elasticized cap sleeves. And it had a bib—an apron?—this shocking white doily thing affixed to the front with a tiny little rosebud near the shoulder. I was mortified. I tried to explain to her that it was a Friday evening, that everyone else would just be wearing the clothes they'd worn to school earlier in the day, that not a single one of my classmates was going to show up in lacy white anklets and black patent leather mary janes. "This isn't a fancy party!" I insisted, eyes brimming with tears, sitting on the kitchen stool as she wrestled my hair into neat pigtails. She was smoking an unfiltered cigarette no-handed, her cherry-red lacquered nails clicking next to my ear as she braided. She didn't respond as she turned my head to survey her craftsmanship. Satisfied, she handed me my good church coat.

"Maybe no one else will show up," I thought, standing on the porch of this gigantic South Evanston mansion with my finger hovering over the doorbell as my mom idled at the curb in her dark green Chevelle. I clutched a bag of imitation Oreo cookies tightly to my chest under my coat. How could she send me to this nice neighborhood with motherfucking Hydrox?! Everyone would know that we were poor and that we had shitty taste in snack foods! I was just about to look for a place to hide them when the front door flew open. "Hi, Samantha!" Reggie's mom trilled, pulling me into her arms for a hug. A hug made hella uncomfortable by the weird contortionist moves I attempted so she wouldn't hear the crinkling of cellophane beneath my jacket. After awkwardly navigating a Christian side hug (aw yeah, my little freshly combed head all up in her armpit!) she ushered me inside the cavernous entryway and offered to take my fancy dress coat. Feeling the weight of those cheap sandwich cookies nestled against my belly, I declined, pretending instead that I was chilly.

The other kids had already arrived and were up on the third floor, and I politely commented on how nice all the expensive furniture and tapestries were as we passed them. I didn't know shit about armoires and credenzas, but I did know that BITCHES NEED COMPLIMENTS. Compliments are the currency of womanhood, and this is one of the many things you learn growing up with a woman who was nearly forty when she gave birth to you. Other things you learn: what Icy Hot smells like, for real; the proper use of Olay night cream; how to fashion a maxi pad out of a kitchen towel because your postmenopausal mother wasn't prepared for you to get your period in the fifth goddamned grade.

She led me up the winding staircase to the second floor, then opened the door to a narrower one. "Up you go!" she said cheerfully, pointing up the stairs. I closed the door behind me as softly as I could before tiptoeing up the creaky stairs. I could hear the hoots and hollers of my classmates ricocheting off the walls above my head, and I slowed my steps. I liked these kids well enough, sure. And they liked me just as well. And it had been a losing argument trying to explain to my mother how you could like people and those same people could like you back, yet going to a party with them that hadn't been mandated by a teacher and was taking place outside of school was akin to pure torture. "Remember when you went to that ice-cream social for the kids who read the most books?" she countered. "You went to *that*. And *that* was a party." And yes, I *had* gone to that. But eating boxed ice cream with M&M's drooling lurid red and blue streaks down its melting heaps with the four other nerds who'd admitted to reading ten or more books in a month hardly qualified as a party, especially since it was hosted at a table in the lunchroom while everyone else either scoffed or glared at us. That ice cream had tasted like loneliness and getting pushed off the swings. But at least there was no kissing.

All I had to do to get out of going was recount to my mother the spin-the-bottle rumor. My mom was an OLD MOM, definitely not a COOL MOM. Everyone liked her because she would just randomly show up in the middle of class with bags of gummy bears and shit, which mortified me to no end. She would drive kids home and invite them for dinner and let them hang out in the tiny apartment I was ashamed we lived in. I just wanted her to stay in our living room, with her cane and her limping and the weird way the multiple sclerosis sometimes rendered her speech, so I could fake like I was normal. My teachers loved her because, through a concerted, meticulous effort to shelter me from absolutely everything, she had produced an overly polite, sensitive little human whose only wish was to be coddled and patted on the head; and she would write "moo juice" on the envelope she tucked into my pocket once a week that contained my milk money, and everyone found that ridiculously clever. I could read at two and entered kindergarten at four, and when my mom divorced my dad that year, my first year of real school, she explained it to me as one would an adult, albeit a tiny one. We became a team. And I got used to listening to a middle-aged broad bitch about her life.

But she wasn't cool, at least not in the way that would've let her ignore the fact that a bunch of kids were going to be licking and blindly groping each other without adult supervision. I knew that, after she banned me from stepping outside our front door ever again, she would get on the phone (or, holy fuck,

GO OVER THERE) and alert those unfit parents to what their spoiled, unruly child was up to. And then I could never go to school ever again. Also, I didn't care that *they* would be kissing; I just didn't want to stand awkwardly in the corner making out with the potato chips because no one in attendance wanted to kiss *me*. So I took one for the fucking team (you're welcome, jerks), and this is where that got me: crouching in the attic stairs, listening to the happy shrieks of a handful of my popular class-mates and wondering how long before I had to pee.

A few minutes passed and I tiptoed up to the landing and peered around a corner through the cracked door. I saw the snack table piled high with boxes of thin-crust cheese pizza (the cur-rency of adolescence), cans of orange pop—OH MY GOD WE GET TO HAVE OUR OWN INDIVIDUAL CANS OF POP! WHAT IS THIS MAGICAL PLACE, OZ?!—and packages of real Oreo cookies. I edged closer to the door, trying to get a look at who was inside while clutching those stupid Hydrox carefully against my belly. So many carefree cool kids, terrifying in their ability to communicate with each other without stam-mering and sweating their shirt sheer.

I dropped to my knees and crawled close enough to the open door that if I stretched my arm out a little bit I could *just barely* graze the back of Danny H's hooded sweatshirt with my finger-tips. I was conflicted: stand up, dust myself off, and announce myself to a roomful of people who scared the shit out of me, in my ill-fitting Easter dress from last year, or hide in the stairwell eating off-brand chocolate sandwich cookies until it was time for my mom to come get me? How I would explain my huddled presence to the kids barreling down the stairs toward the fleet of awaiting minivans hadn't yet occurred to my tiny brain. Muffled talk of bottles for spinning echoed out into the hallway, and I knew that the window for a non-awkward entrance had just slammed shut. The thought of some terrified boy skittering out of the way of the nozzle of a two-liter Coke bottle I'd set into motion was enough to make my stomach churn, so I stood up as quietly as I could and tiptoed down the stairs.

Reggie's mom was in the kitchen, squinting at a crossword puzzle in the newspaper over her reading glasses while the opening theme from *Wheel of Fortune* blared from the small television affixed to the underside of the cabinet. I squealed with glee, and she patted the stool next to hers. "This is my favorite show," I gushed, scrambling into the seat, thrilled at the opportunity to impress a woman fancy enough TO HAVE A MOTHERFUCKING TELEVISION IN HER GOD-DAMNED KITCHEN. I was one of those precocious, know-it-all children: volunteering facts and figures and unsolicited answers, totally gross in my adorable smart-aleckiness. I couldn't wait to show off how much random shit I knew; my mom and I watched *Jeopardy!*, *Family Feud*, *The Price Is Right*, and *Wheel* religiously. There was a notepad on the coffee table with the tallies of each afternoon's game show scores. I always won, because I had a very nice mother who would intentionally tank her answers during the Fast Money round, but she didn't have to because you would seriously have to be an idiot to not know that "washing dishes" is the answer sixty-two out of one hundred surveyed people will give to the question "What household chore do husbands hate the most?"

I've always been comfortable with moms. Every sleepover, when I was the first to fall asleep at 7:30 p.m. in the guest room while all the other kids stayed up until midnight giggling in the basement, I would be awake at dawn and in the kitchen, watching the mom brew coffee and pour my orange juice. Every birthday party, while all the other kids tore ass around Showbiz shrieking at a deafening volume and raucously playing arcade games, I would volunteer to stand guard over the gift table, talking about mom stuff with the moms. My own mom was a nurse, and kind of old, and she couldn't get around very well, so when she wasn't sleeping all day after working overnights in the ER, she hardly had the energy to kick a ball around with me. I was good at all the inside stuff: crocheting afghans, making chicken stock and bologna sandwiches, raising baby kittens, staying on top of every plot twist on *General Hospital*.

Even now, moms totally fucking love me. I'm like a spoonful of Jif with a multivitamin sprinkled on top. If I meet your mom, even for a second, she's going to fall head over heels in love with me. I'm not even sure how it happens. Our eyes lock over a box of wine or a pot of decaf afternoon coffee; we smile shyly, toying with the hems of our Talbots lightweight knit cardigans; then, finally, an embrace: gentle, mindful of our creaky hips and aching knees, shrouded in the heady ambrosia created by the Tiger Balm applied liberally to our painful joints and muscles, quick to account for our raging hormonal heat.

I like underwear that I can pull all the way up to my tits, and I like eating room-temperature soup at four in the afternoon, and I guess what I'm trying to say is that I understand your mom. I mean, I *get* her, which is why we watched *Criminal Minds* last week while updating her online dating profile. Young motherfuckers are loud and poor and make for *terrible* trivia partners. Okay, sure, she texts me in ALL CAPS and comments on every single hilarious post I make on Facebook with "HIHoney!" or asks, "Sam, dear, how are your hemorrhoids doing?" on my

Instagram, but I don't care, because she doesn't mind hanging out watching Lifetime movies on a Friday night, and when I ask her to make me a Tom Collins she (1) knows what the hell that even means, and (2) already has the ingredients to make that shit.

My mom is dead. And, if she were alive, I'd probably be like, "OH MY GOD, BITCH, GET THE FUCK OFF TWITTER."

She ain't, though, but she left behind a perfectly groomed fifty-two-year-old woman to carry on her legacy. All I ever want to do is make podiatrist appointments and find professional-looking pajama pants that I can pass off as actual clothing. I want soft shoes and elasticized waistbands and a boyfriend who is happy enough to just drive me around to run my errands and won't inspect my birthmarks too closely. I'm basically your weird aunt who sends you $5 gift cards to places you would never shop. Bitches my age are too loud and too text message–y, and I don't understand their fashion choices. I'm totally fluent in Mom, and I guess what I'm really trying to say is that I'm dating you to get closer to that hot broad who won't stop showing up unannounced at your apartment pretending to drop off mail you couldn't care less about when really she just wants to snoop around and make sure you've purchased laundry detergent. Don't get mad at me, bro, I just really love laughing wistfully over salads or whatever it is premenopausal women are always doing in commercials for adult diapers. LET ME TAKE YOUR MOM OUT FOR SCONES.

Reggie's mom and I ate the pizza she had ordered for herself (artichokes and olives and other *very grown-up things*), and I still got my VERY OWN CAN OF POP. We picked our players and kept score on a greasy napkin, and I tried not to shout too loud or jump out of my chair when I solved the final puzzle using only a *P* and an *L* because I still had those stupid fucking cookies hidden beneath my coat. She talked to me about mom stuff: groceries and laundry and children and fatigue. We talked about school and we talked about boys and we talked about my upcoming piano recital and we watched half of a made-for-TV movie and then my sister was on the porch, ringing the bell to collect me, earlier than everyone else's designated drivers by an hour. I ran up the stairs to our apartment and my mom asked how the party was and I shouted, "Fun!" while streaking past her to my bedroom to get out of my suffocating coat and those uncomfortably tiny patent leather shoes.

I kicked off the shoes and hurled my coat into the closet and that package of Hydrox hit the wood floor with a thud. I burst out laughing and shoved as many into my mouth as would fit and tucked the still-warm package beneath my pillow for my late-night undercover-reading snack. I scrambled into my pajamas hoping that there was still time left for me to watch both *Hunter* and *Amen*, key components of our Friday-night ritual. My mom liked those shows, so I liked them, too. *LA Law*, all that shit. She was talking on the phone with one of her church friends, crochet needles clicking staccato as she chatted. I glanced at the notepad on the table with our *Wheel of Fortune* scorecard and recalled my earlier game. I picked up the pencil as my mom eyed me warily over the magnifying glasses she bought once a week at Walgreens because she was always losing them. "Mrs. L $1,850, Samantha $2,750 + a trip to the Bahamas," I printed in my meticulous script. "Still undefeated!" I beamed, momentarily forgetting that I had eight black sandwich cookies crammed between my cheeks. "You are in big trouble," Mom mouthed, pointing at the evidence of my crime as I drooled a trail of dark crumbs down the front of my pink nightgown. But I knew I wouldn't be. "I can sweet-talk my way out of anything with her," I thought as I pulled off her Dr. Scholl's and started massaging her bony toes. I'm totally adorable. And moms totally fucking love me.

my mother, my daughter

My mother became my daughter when I was nine years old. There had been an accident, a car accident, and it was a bad one, although I didn't know that yet. My heartbeat quickened when I rounded the corner onto our street and noticed that the creaky, rusted-out Dodge we couldn't afford to keep gas in wasn't parked in front of our crumbling apartment complex. Permission to walk to and from school had been hard won; my mother was careful with me and overprotective in the extreme, resulting in a young girl who was incredibly naive and grossly underdeveloped emotionally. I wet the bed, I cried at the slightest provocation, and I entertained myself with a steady stream of fantasies and daydreams, rarely connecting with the outside world. So we made a deal: I could walk myself home from school if I promised not to dawdle and play along the way, and if

I wasn't on the threshold of our building by 3:35 she would get in the car and come looking for me.

I didn't wear a watch, because watches were for grown-ups, of course, and I wasn't even allowed to have my own key. So I broke into a run, thinking I might be able to catch her before she got too far away and my newfound privileges were revoked for good. But I hadn't even stopped at the corner store for candy! I didn't roll around on the ground with that puppy down the street like I'd wanted to! How could I possibly be late?! Maybe her clock was set faster than the one at school?! There was no sign of the car in either direction, so I turned around and dragged my sorry ass home, savoring what was sure to be the last few minutes of freedom I was going to be granted for the fore-seeable future.

I found her standing in the tiny yellow kitchen sipping a cup of coffee, the instant kind that you mix with hot water that was sold in a gallon-size drum for two dollars at the dollar store and that smelled like cat urine. One side of her head was ban-daged, and there were some deep lacerations on her face. She explained that she'd fallen asleep while driving and had been blindsided by another car. My mom hadn't been wearing a seat belt and was thrown across the front seat of the car, smacking her head pretty hard against the rearview mirror in the pro-cess. There had been an ambulance and a trip to the emergency room. The Dodge was totaled. All while I was working on my stupid spelling worksheet.

I had been her first accident, or so it seemed to everyone but my parents. It just didn't seem logical to anyone of sound mind that two people rapidly degenerating through middle age down a sharp, slippery slope into the pit of senior citizenship would make the choice to have a baby. "Why not get another dog?" her friends asked. "Maybe you guys could travel . . . ?" My father, at fifty, had recently survived his second heart attack, and my mother, ten years his junior, had been diagnosed with multiple sclerosis four years prior. But "remission" is one of those magical words, one of those words that makes *anything* seem possible, and once her neurologist uttered it, she decided that it was time to soldier onward and give birth to her fourth and final child. The obstetrician warned her against it, saying that I would surely be born with Down syndrome or some other form of mental retardation. He pointed out that she wasn't in the best physical condition, that pregnancy and childbirth were going to further ravage a body that was long past its childbearing prime.

The day after the accident started out like any other. I had the day off from school courtesy of one Jewish holiday or another, a perk of growing up in the suburbs, and to show my gratitude I kicked the covers off and bounded out of bed early to get a jump on my cartoon watching and cereal eating. My mom was generally an early riser, up at five every morning even though the progressing multiple sclerosis had forced her to retire a couple of years before, but she was sound asleep next to me. I assumed she just needed to sleep in, that she wasn't up yelling at me to take a bath and put real clothes on because the accident had worn her out, making her more tired than usual. So I tiptoed out of the bedroom and went to fill a salad bowl with cereal. I sat on the couch in a Cinnamon Toast Crunch coma until the cartoons gave way to boring talk shows, which reminded me that I still hadn't heard so much as a peep out of my mom. She was sitting on the side of the bed we shared, eyes unfocused, drooling and unresponsive.

A childhood that had begun with a sort of cautious optimism quickly devolved into absolute horseshit. My father was an abusive alcoholic, a man tormented by the demons he'd brought home with him after fighting the war in Korea. He'd tempered his rage for most of their marriage, but after two failed stints in rehab, he gave up and caved completely, drowning himself in liquor and taking his anger out on everyone around him. My mom and I left the idyllic three-story home into which I'd been born when I was four and shared one shitty Section 8 apartment after another with mice and roaches, relegated to surviving on food stamps, Social Security, and other forms of government aid. She could no longer work thanks to her rapidly deteriorating body and brain and spent most of her waking hours smoking cigarettes and gambling away the little bit of money we had on lottery tickets.

I went next door to get the neighbor, because we never had enough money to keep a phone on. I should explain that I grew up in a wealthy, progressive community. That, while there were these pockets of poverty and tragedy scattered throughout our town, my experience didn't mirror those of the majority of my classmates. That I was expected to keep my fucking shit together and learn the goddamned state capitals, terrified that my mom was going to drown in the bathtub as I struggled to grasp the concept of halves and thirds. I didn't yet understand the difference between God and the president, yet I knew which pills went with breakfast and which ones were taken after dinner.

I went to sleepovers without a sleeping bag and marveled at my classmates' novelty pillows and Jem paraphernalia. They had fathers at home and multicar garages and college funds and MOTHERFUCKING TELEPHONES, and here I was hurtling up and down three flights of stairs desperately pounding on doors that wouldn't open because normal people had jobs, healthy people actually left their apartments during the day to venture out into the world and accomplish real things. Finally one of the doors creaked open, and I breathlessly tried to explain, using my limited nine-year-old language, that my mother had a disease in her brain and had been in a bad car crash and now wouldn't answer me when I asked her if everything was okay.

I sat in the waiting room with the kind of faceless authority figure who sits with your child when you are her only person, in my pajamas, milk spilled down the front, urine staining the crotch, reading *Harriet the Spy* and completely unaware of the major shift occurring beneath the tectonic plates of my life. There was a blood clot in her brain, at the site of impact, and the doctors had to shave her head and crack her skull open to get it out before it ruptured and killed her. And they did, which was a kind of little miracle.

I brought my baby home from the hospital a few days later, swaddled at the wrong end, head and neck wrapped in thick white gauze and cotton pads. There was a long, red, angry-looking scar snaking its way from the left side of her forehead over her ear and coming to an end at the base of her skull. I would learn over the course of the days, weeks, and months to come how to mask how much I was hurting. How to hide how badly we were struggling to survive from the nosy social worker the teachers kept pulling me out of class to see, the man in the ill-fitting suit who spoke to me in his most gentle inside voice while silently judging my missing socks and uncombed hair. The woman who used fancy words to try to trick me into admitting that my home environment was unsafe, that I was living with a person who could no longer properly take care of me. She pushed me to betray a woman trapped in a baby body she couldn't use who had done nothing but love me and try her hardest to make me feel special, to admit that I had no idea what abandoned building my father was currently drinking himself to death in. Didn't this bitch know that I was stressed the fuck out? Wasn't it clear that I had been up half the night changing my mother's diaper and helping her into and out of the bed, and that's why I couldn't stay awake in science class? Yes, social studies is boring, but that isn't why I'm not paying attention; I'm thinking about how I have to run to the currency exchange when school lets out to make a ComEd payment so our lights don't get shut off again. Will the nice dude who works at White Hen be there today? He knows that the cigarettes aren't for me, he won't give me a hard time, and maybe I'll have enough left over for a Snapple since I didn't use my milk quarter at lunch today. No, I didn't have time to do everything in my goddamned homework packet, dudes. I have a lot of shit on my mind! Don't you know I have a baby at home who is depending on me?

Here is how multiple sclerosis is explained to you when you are a young child: "Okay, Samantha, I want you to think of your brain as a series of wires. Can you picture it?" I remember wanting very badly to impress the neurologist because I needed him to understand that I was totally responsible enough to be in charge of my baby's care, even though I peed the bed the last three nights and cried in the bathroom when no one had anything nice to say about my diorama, so I nodded assuredly. "Now, this disease your mommy has is called multiple sclerosis"—he waited while I repeated it back to him—"and what it does is it attacks the coating on those wires. It just eats it up, like candy. Right now it's working on the wires that control Grace's legs, and that's why she's having trouble standing up and walking around. And eventually it will eat the coating on her arm wires, and her talking wires, and her thinking wires." It had been two years since her accident, and the brain damage left behind by having her head cracked open had accelerated the aggressiveness of the MS, basically rendering her an invalid who never left the squalor of our tiny apartment. I watched her pushing a borrowed walker around his office, her brain a makeshift arcade that housed only an outdated *Pac-Man* machine. *Chomp chomp chomp chomp.* She bumped clumsily into the chair I was sitting in. *Chomp chomp chomp.* High score.

I had to get my fucking shit together. It didn't take long for me to realize that the worse of a job I did keeping myself clean and getting myself out of bed to get to places on time and finishing my assignments by the time they were due, the more frequently my day was interrupted by various school authorities demanding to know who was in charge of my care and why they were doing such a shitty fucking job. I knew that if I wore the same underwear for three days someone would notice how I smelled and alert the teacher, or that if I put my head down for more than a second that I would have to explain to the principal why I was so tired all the time. So I stopped.

We lived like college kids: ramen noodles, cheap hot dogs, instant coffee, grape Kool-Aid. I was responsible for the shopping, which I did every week at the corner store down the street from our newest place. We had moved again so that we could be closer to the fire station, because there still wasn't enough money for a phone and if I needed to run down there in the middle of the night and get help, I could. There was a bench for sitting and a bar installed in the shower, and a raised toilet seat to make it easier for my mom to do things for herself during the day while I was at school. I had been taking piano lessons since I was four, and we finally had space for a piano. I didn't even know Mom had been putting money away, but I came home one afternoon to find an upright that was easily nine hundred years old and about to collapse on itself in the middle of the living room, and she was so happy, thrilled to death and so fucking proud that she was able to be the mom again that it nearly broke my heart. I played an entire book of Bach concertos while she listened with her eyes closed and tried to move along with the music.

Most people get fifty or sixty years of life to prepare for what I was struggling to cope with after only eleven: Did Mom eat today? Is it okay if I leave the house for more than an hour? Will she remember to take her pills at the right time today? What happens if she tries to leave the house again? And I had to balance this shit against equally important issues like: How badly are they going to make fun of me for wearing fake Keds? Do I have the right Trapper Keeper? What if that boy in band finds out I have a crush on him? Because you don't just get to withdraw from your child life while making sure that your disabled mother doesn't set the apartment on fire because her fingers can no longer close firmly around a cigarette. There is no opt-out button on adolescence. I would divide myself into two people: the happy, smiling person who needed to make friends and appear to be having a well-adjusted childhood during the day, and my mother's mother and nursemaid and caretaker and friend at night. I had sisters, but they were busy with their own lives, real grown-ups with children of their own to tend to, and none of them could shoulder the burden of two more babies to care for. So we tried to do it on our own.

It's my fault that she was taken away from me. I was selfish, and I failed her, and I remain haunted by that to this day. It was my first year of high school, and I so desperately wanted to have some semblance of normalcy in my life. It was palpable, this dull ache of yearning. I was tired, and my life had never been my own, and I wanted so badly to just do the things that other kids got to do. My suicide note was brief, one big weak apology, and I left it on my desk and took as many of her pills as I could. I just kept swallowing and swallowing them until I couldn't anymore, and then I lay down in my bed and passed out. My little baby was so sad when she found me, called to motherhood this one last time, and she woke me up and poured baking powder mixed with hot water down my throat to make me vomit. She couldn't walk down the block to get me an ambulance, and I was too sick and embarrassed to go get my own, so I got in the shower and threw up down the drain until I felt empty. That was on Saturday, and the following Monday I got up early to go to school to rehearse with the jazz band before first period. After the final bell rang I hung out with some friends, doing nothing, even though I knew I should get home to make sure my mother was okay. But I resented her, I resented these constraints that were locked tight around what should have otherwise been a thirteen-year-old life of fun and freedom. So I took my sweet fucking time, savoring every stolen minute.

My daughter was lying on the floor just inside the door. She had fallen nearly twelve hours before, trying to make her way from her chair in the living room to the bathroom a few minutes after I'd left to get the bus. She was lying on her stomach in a sickening pool of her own waste, voice hoarse from spending hours calling for help, eyes red and out of tears. I tried to get her up, because she pulled me to the floor and begged me to, because I'm sure she knew that this was the end, that our jig was about to be up, that if I couldn't get her up and into bed that finally someone was going to come and take me away. And I tried to, I really did. I got down on my knees and slipped and slid in my baby's urine and feces, trying to figure out an angle at which I could prop her up so that I could slide something under her and get her to her feet. If only we knew our neighbors better, if only I could call someone to help me, if only I hadn't been a selfish fucking bitch who thought it was more important to hang around the park with this group of idiot popular kids who were all completely oblivious to my existence than it was to get home to my mother four hours earlier than I did, maybe this would have turned out a different way. But I could feel the plates shifting yet again.

I couldn't get her up by myself, no matter how hard I tried, and her leg wires had been completely destroyed, leaving her helpless on her own behalf, so I dropped my backpack in the hall and tore down the street to the fire department, tracking Mom's shit the length of the sidewalk. I threw my shoes into a garbage can on the street as I watched them bring the gurney down the short flight of stairs that had been one of the major factors in our choice of this particular building. That and the landlord's acceptance of rent vouchers. Mom spent a week in the hospital while people with clipboards and stern faces made decisions about what was going to happen to this child I had spent the last four years caring for and, for that matter, what was going to happen to me. Like most concerned mothers, I slept in the lounge chair next to her bed, waking up every few hours when the nurse came in to check my baby girl's vitals. I tucked the blankets in around her after they messed them up with all their blood-pressure checks and blood draws, filled the pitcher with ice chips from the kitchen area on the other side of the hospital wing, pressed the call button when she needed another injection of pain medication and couldn't reach it for herself. I was her only person.

For the five years that it took my daughter to die, all I could think about was how I'd do anything to take her place. That life had dealt this lovely, gentle creature a bad hand she'd done nothing to deserve, and meanwhile I hadn't done very much with the handful of years already under my belt. I wasn't pretty; I wasn't very good at much other than the piano; why not give her the rest of these years to do something with? It was excruciating, watching what had once been a vibrant and beautiful flower wilt and dehydrate in slow motion. I had to take three buses after school to get to the nursing home she was placed in, and I did so as often as I could while trying not to fail out of high school, writing her name in black Sharpie on all her rapidly disappearing belongings, making sure that her pillows were fluffed the way she liked them, and painting her nails red even though they always got chipped during occupational therapy. I brought her bags of jelly beans from the gas station and talked to her about all the kid shit I had been too busy to get around to before: boys I had crushes on, the chemistry teacher I hated with the fire of a thousand suns. But who gives a fuck about my floundering GPA when I can't be there to stop them from hitting her when she doesn't move fast enough? Who gives a shit about how terrible the cafeteria food is when she can't stop my borrowed family from mistreating me?

Fourteen years have passed since the day I sat at the foot of yet another hospital bed, watching the morphine that would end my mother's life drip slowly into her arm, robbing her first of consciousness, then of breath. My father had been found dead and homeless, frozen in the street, six months before. Fourteen years since the doctor said that the lung infection was going to kill her in a matter of days anyway, that between the MS and the dementia, at fifty-five years young this gaunt skeleton whose skin hung from her skull like wet laundry was a shell of her former radiant self, and at that point it was obviously the most humane thing to do.

My mom had worn dentures her whole life because she'd been severely abused as a child and had never been given milk, causing all her adult teeth to rot and fall out of her head by the time she was in the eighth grade. She never went anywhere without them, not ever, but sometimes, before she tucked me in at night, she would take them out and grab her cane and pretend to be the witch in *Snow White* until I was laughing so hard I couldn't fall asleep. After she was pronounced dead, the doctor removed her teeth and set them in a pan on the bedside table before they wheeled her down to the morgue, and as I leaned over the side rail to memorize her face one last time, it only then occurred to me how without them she didn't really look like a witch; she mostly just looked like a baby.

What can you possibly do with the rest of your life when this is how it begins? Who am I supposed to be? When do I get the manual on how to be an adult or what everything means? How am I supposed to build a life on the wreckage that is this foundation? How can I be sure those plates won't shift?!

Children should never die before their parents.

the triplets

When I was nineteen I lived in a fucking crack house. Both of my parents had died the year before, and I chose to drop out of Northern Illinois University (where I had spent the last semester of my studies watching *Braveheart* every single day and eating ice-cream sandwiches in bed) and jettisoned a potentially exciting life filled with hanging around frat parties to which I had not been formally invited, to instead rent a room in a split-level ranch house in a decent neighborhood that had been repurposed from moderately attractive single family home to fully functioning crack house and possible bordello. My sole possessions, in order of value and/or importance: (1) a rusted-out 1988 Ford Escort, hatchback, stick shift, that I'd purchased with the $700 that remained of my father's meager life insurance payout; (2) three uncashed Social Security checks, in my name, which is the dead-parent silver lining; (3) an eighty-eight-key electric piano and an operational key-tar; (4) a box of "impressive" works of literature; and (5) a bag of pharmaceutical-grade heroin I was planning to eventually kill myself with. I was living the dream.

I had a job selling doughnuts at a bakery in Evanston, Illinois, where I grew up. You haven't *lived* until you've had to sell apple fritters to your high school classmates home on spring break from Yale. The money you make doing a job like that is fucking laughable, and I supplemented my income housesitting, walking dogs, and selling prescription drugs and FDA-disapproved diet pills to your mom. The crack house was the best a person with *no* job history, *no* cosigner, *no* credit score, *no* references, and *no* bank account could come up with in a jam. I'd responded to a handwritten ad in the coffee shop I would hang out in when I got sick of eating leftover Danish for dinner, all the gross flavors like apricot and prune that NOBODY EVER FUCKING BUYS. When I went to check it out, the mellow atmosphere of the house *definitely* appealed to my, ahem, bohemian sensibilities. I have always been the type of person who takes her shoes off no matter where I happen to be; long skirts, Earth Shoes, woven bags: this was my uniform in the late fucking nineties.

During the "tour," which basically consisted of a glance into the communal bathroom and a quick peek at the kitchen, I was impressed by how laid-back all the other tenants seemed. The house had clearly once belonged to a nice family who loved it, as evidenced by the sunny-yellow curtains and carefully arranged flowerpots just outside the front door. It was unclear to me whether those people who'd installed heated bathroom tiles had fallen on hard times and were the same ones who'd resorted to selling neatly packaged Baggies of coke and weed out of the back door, or if they'd jumped ship as the property value plummeted around them and were now wallpapering a new house in a less-shitty part of town with 100 percent fewer strung-out kids on PCP peppering their lawn. The landlord and I stepped over an unconscious dude clutching a forty in the hallway outside of what was to be my bedroom. "I'll *totally* take it," I said as he handed me a padlock and a key. "Dude, everyone is so fucking *relaxed* here."

I came home one night a few weeks later to find a basehead helping himself to my belongings. After the indignity of having to wrestle a motherfucking Dave Matthews Band CD from the clutches of a GROWN-ASS MAN, I decided to pack my shit and fend for myself like a feral cat out on the streets.

For three months I slept in the backseat of my tiny car and showered with dusty bars of low-quality soap in hourly motels. Then I moved in with my friend's stepdad, a recently divorced photographer and graphic designer who took pity on my functional homelessness and offered me both a job and Jon's childhood bedroom. And that is humbling in the most excruciatingly uncomfortable way, sleeping surrounded by the remnants of someone else's happy childhood. But it was a bed, and it was safe. And I know that totally sounds sketchy and dirtbaggedy, moving in with some grody old dude who wasn't married to my friend's mom anymore, but his offer was the most genuine and selfless kindness I'd received in a really long fucking time.

I spent my days ordering catered lunches for photo shoots and peering through a magnifying loupe at slides on a light box like I really knew what the fuck I was looking at. I answered the phone, cropped and outlined photos, and edited sentences describing stainless steel sauté pans. I am surprisingly charming on the telephone, and I can learn just about anything, so after two weeks of watching me eat $15 sandwiches and proposition-ing the Calumet delivery dudes who came every day to pick up film, Mel decided his money would be way better spent sending my ass to design school in order to hone my burgeoning design skills.

The school was called Mac University. It was not a real school. Housed in a painfully hip two-story loft building in the middle of that pseudo-industrial district on Halsted Street just north of Chicago Avenue, this was essentially a trade school for computer geeks, the kind of assholes who referred to their G5s as "supe-rior machines" and sat around comparing gigs of RAM in a *Revenge of the Nerds*–style dick-measuring contest. I was awed by the slick hardwood floors, Snapple vending machines, and track lighting and terrified by these mysterious hipster nerds who discussed LARPing during the class breaks and the coked-out junior PR executives whose bosses were forcing them to learn Photoshop and who only ate a third of the Lean Cuisines they'd brought for lunch. This is the kind of dumb shit I notice, that a bitch the circumference of my forearm took two bites out of a low-fat cheese enchilada and carelessly wasted the remaining two hundred calories and three unused Weight Watchers points down the garbage disposal in the communal kitchen.

I had stress diarrhea from the beginning. With my hoodies and my Birkenstocks and my saddle bags I just *did not* fit in with these people and their designer sunglasses and asymmetrical hair-cuts. And they made sure I fucking knew it; these dicks totally iced me the fuck out. No one asked if I wanted anything from the vending machine at the start of the class. No one wanted to know what kind of job I did in my real life. I'm not even sure that anyone other than the instructor, this smarmy dirtbag who spent half the class trying to solicit his most attractive students, knew my goddamned name. Until they saw the car.

The most interesting thing about the male midlife crisis is that, at its core, it is less about the looming fear of manhood lost than it is about letting your inner thirteen-year-old run around doing all the shit he couldn't do when he didn't yet have credit cards. Mel and I drank wine every day and ate five-star dinners every night and pretty much wiped our asses with $100 bills in between. Unshackled from his second wife, he was living life the way it deserves to be fucking lived. And before I met that dude I didn't know shit about sparkling water or Jacuzzi bathtubs or Pratesi sheets. I didn't know what Ezekiel bread was. Or that there are more than four types of cheese. I got a nearly perfect score on the ACT but had no idea that people actually ate uncooked vegetables that weren't salad.

I sold my Escort for fifty bucks and a couple of handfuls of muscle relaxers because my new dad had a bunch of shiny new toys I could drive, the most impressive of which was a gigantic Mercedes-Benz sedan. It was one of those wide-bodied E series, the 320: buttery leather interior, black on black, sunroof, power everything, CD changer in the trunk. COME ON, asshole, it was 1999! Before cars could call an ambulance for you or suck your dick while waiting in line at the drive-thru! So THAT CAR WAS BALLER. Seriously, it had the biggest testicles on the road. My official job title was something between "amateur accountant" and "struggling, inattentive copy editor," but mostly I just drove that pussy wagon around all day picking up Prada suits from the dry cleaner and grocery shopping for things like bok choy and millet. It suited me, this life of personal assistant/

adopted daughter. At that point in my life I felt *so uncared for*, and pretending Mel was my father while ordering his double espressos made me feel like we were a little family.

I'd been in the class for two weeks, getting A's on all of my art projects BECAUSE I'M A GODDAMNED GENIUS while alternately trying to blend into the wallpaper and apologizing for my grossly unflattering T.J.Maxx pants with my big "I'm sorry I'm poor" eyes, when the ground beneath my social palatability shifted for the better. The Quark workshop I was taking ran from 5:00 to 9:00 p.m., and like clockwork every Tuesday and Thursday at 8:55, I would gather my things, slip unnoticed from my seat at the back of the room, then drive as far south as I could on Lake Shore Drive looking at the twinkling city lights before turning around and driving all the way back to Jon's bedroom in the suburbs. But this week I was doing a cleanse, another crazy rich-white-person thing, and all that lemon water was making me shit green diarrhea like you would not believe. At nine fifteen I stepped out of the school building, into a group of my classmates, who were smoking cigarettes in that glamorous style of the perpetually bored and indifferent. They weren't paying attention to me but I waved anyway. This little dirtbag hooker wearing a goddamned miniskirt to fucking learn Photoshop asked if I was going to get on the bus, and I pointed to the car, that gleaming hulk of German steel, and said, "I have my car." And then I left in it.

Our homework assignment had been to mock up a three-page brochure. Mine was about the exhilarating world of stainless steel measuring cups. Working in an actual studio afforded me the luxury of high-quality print materials, and I reveled in my newfound rock stardom as everyone oohed and aahed over my full-color glossy photographs. This salty-ass Asian broad whom

I knew from her incessant fucking bragging and who was a FANCY AND SUPER-IMPORTANT intern at the Art Institute stood at the edge of the table, lips pursed, scowling at my work. "Whose car were you driving last week?" she asked aggressively. What a fucking cunt. Thirty-two-year-old Sam would've told that smug bitch to GET ON MY FUCKING DICK, but at nineteen I was meek and hesitant and easily intimidated, so I just sat there in stunned silence feeling the heat of embarrassment creeping up my neck. What is this, ninth-grade gym class? And I had just ducked out of the way of the volleyball speeding toward my face? Was I really going to sit there cowed by a woman wearing inappropriately youthful footwear?! NO, I WAS NOT.

"That's my husband's car. He's a doctor." The lie came out so smoothly and felt so good in my mouth that I repeated it again. "I have a husband, and he is a doctor." I looked at all the expectant eyes surrounding me. Are they buying this shit? Like, for real? There's gravy on my fucking shirt! "What hospital?" asked one. "What is his specialty?" asked another. And with that, I lost my goddamned mind. With a rapt audience of twenty-four assholes who up until that moment had acted as if they hated me at a cellular level, I spun a fairy tale of epic proportion featuring my wealthy, Aryan German doctor husband (Mercedes come from Germany, right?) who performed hours of complicated brain surgeries during the day (naturally) and who was also a loving and attentive father to our children every night (well, of course). He just so happened to be a fantastic cook (right), played tennis all weekend to stay in incredible shape (sure), and even had sex with me when I was on my period (what a saint!). These soulless dummies who'd been mean to me because of my shoes ate that shit up with a spoon. "How many kids do you have?" chirped one girl and, drunk on the command I had over these ridiculous jerks, I said, "*Six.*"

I'm not really sure why I said that. Two sets of triplets, all male, conceived in a laboratory I'd seen in an episode of *The X-Files*. My sexual activity up to that point had been limited to two incredibly awkward and equally embarrassing experiences: first, the loss of my virginity five years prior, in the laundry room of my sister's apartment building to this douchebag I went to high school with who had a fucking S-Curl and actually WORE AN ELECTRIC BLUE SUIT TO CLASS every Friday for spirit day; then, six months before, I let the overnight muffin-and-bread dude fuck me in the asshole behind a Hobart mixer after work. I didn't have any goddamned babies, and one of those types of intercourse can't even get you pregnant. But I soldiered on, pretending to know what IVF treatments really meant and coming up with names for six German children ON THE GODDAMNED SPOT. (For reference's sake, they were: Kermit, Kaiser, Karl, Konstantin, Konrad, and Kiefer; crossbred for the inception of the hybrid Nazi–Black Panther army I was attempting to sire with my doctor husband, Kurt.)

Blame my wide hips and meatbeard, or maybe my powerful gift for storytelling, but they *believed* me. They really did believe that I had, *shit*, six strapping young men from my oozing womb hole and was now taking a design class to "satisfy my intellectual curiosity." And I couldn't get enough. Every time I came to class someone would ask about "my boys," and I would make up a story about how the nanny burned down the coach house. Or that we'd started our own peewee football team. It didn't even matter what I said; my vagina was a fucking celebrity. I created this fully developed fantasy life, augmented by my access to a fleet of fancy divorce-mobiles and a subscription to *Saveur* magazine, and once I started I just COULD NOT STOP LYING. That attention was addictive, and no one was fact-checking my stories, so I just kept the party going.

Like most junkies, I didn't even see rock bottom coming. The night before our final exam I decided to drink a bottle of Cinzano and make truffles, because that's what rich ladies with six screaming children do, isn't it?! I couldn't find a melon baller to make perfectly round scoops of filling, and I fucked them all the way up. The misshapen piles of what looked like shiny dog turds as I removed them from the freezer would have been an absolute failure to someone less creative but, as I peeled them off the wax paper and attempted to salvage them, a brilliant idea occurred to me. "These look like children made them." I put them in a white paper box and tied a red ribbon around it. And then I sat down at a drafting table and wrote a thank-you note to my classmates, WITH MY LEFT HAND. I am a righty, and not the least bit ambidextrous. I signed it with six little wobbly *K*'s.

I spent the two years following completion of the program designing catalogs and packaging for wholesale food services without incident. Mel went through a rugged-outdoorsman phase and traded his flashy Benz for a couple of Jeeps, and the pitter-patter of tiny imaginary feet came to an end as the last of the people I'd stayed in touch with from that dumb class faded away after two or three e-mails. On my twenty-first birthday a group of my friends went to Lava Lounge, the kind of place that looked like it belonged in a TLC video and was always teeming with the worst possible dudes. Stephanie and I were laughing and shouting into each other's faces the way girls do when we are drunk. "I TOTALLY WANT TO FUCK THE DUDE WITH THE GUMBY SHIRT AND THE FANNY PACK!" "OH MY GOD, THOSE CROSS COLOURS JEANS ARE

SO SEXY!" when I felt an ominous presence looming over us. It was that motherfucking Asian woman, still wearing shoes better suited for a teenage girl, eyeing me skeptically over her cocktail. She asked where my husband was and how my six children were doing, then detailed six months' worth of my lies all while Steph watched in disbelief. "Two sets of triplets? German husband?!" she shrieked. "Doesn't schnitzel give you the runs? You haven't even had that much sex yet! Didn't you just get your driver's license?!" I almost died.

A couple of years ago I finally got up the courage to tell Mel all the lies I'd used his cars and knowledge of fine spirits to perpetuate. He sat across the table from me, brow furrowed, shaking his head disappointedly. Finally, he sighed. "Sam," he said gravely, "I'm not mad that you lied. I'm not even mad that you kind of made me look like a pedophile. I understand why you did it, and I'd understand if you needed to do it again. Just remember next time that I am a MOTHERFUCKING JEW."

this is why i'm poor

I only play the dead-parents card when I ABSOLUTELY HAVE TO. Like when I don't want to go somewhere I hate or do something nice for someone else. ("What do you mean it's my turn to buy a round at the bar?! I CAN'T BUY DRINKS! My parents are DEAD!") Just kidding, in those instances I just become selectively deaf until someone more flush with cash scoots out of the booth to get everybody's shots and beers. Anyway, there are quite a few things this certified adult is incapable of doing, like balancing a checkbook and being fiscally responsible, that serve as concrete evidence that I've had very little adult guidance and supervision since the age of thirteen. To catch up those of you who came late to the party, my parents were sick and too fucking old to have a baby and both died (separately) when I was a teenager, and that's probably why I make so many reckless and terrible decisions. Such as putting the intimate details of my butthole on the Internets.

To my credit, I have had my own apartment and have paid my own way since I was eighteen. To my detriment, I have been solely responsible for my finances since that age, as well. Considering the number of thirty-plus-year-old dudes I know still living at home or still sleeping on some bitch's couch or still subsisting on ramen and potato chips, I'd say I've kept this ship afloat pretty well. I was homeless twice, once at nineteen and again at twenty, but that's only because you can't trust bitches you randomly meet wherever stupid bitches hang out to be good roommates and not get you thrown the fuck out of wherever it is you're living. All this to say that no one ever taught me anything about money. EVER. I mean, we never had any, so what was there ever to teach? I know how to get Social Security benefits and free health care, but no one ever talked to me about retirement or credit scores. I fucked around and almost ended up in jail because I didn't know that not paying taxes for contract work is illegal and IRS fraud. How the fuck was I supposed to know what a goddamned 1099 was?! People assume you have parents or guardians to walk you through that kind of shit. Good thing my crooked-ass lawyer knew the judge.

So it's tax time, and my homeboy was over the other night badgering me about filing a return, asking me about all my receipts and bank statements and whether I saved the checks I used to pay for that class I took. Um . . . yeah, right. I'm sure I either burned that shit or flushed it down the toilet or used it to line Helen Keller's litter box. Save my receipts, for what? To prove to the government how many times I purchased the same exact black sweater at the Gap? Hold on to my bank statements, for whom? To prove how many times I stopped and started and stopped and restarted paying for eHarmony, or whatever? YEAH, RIGHT. Is there some sort of loneliness deduction I don't know about? Some alcoholic tax credit? No? Then get the fuck out of my face with that.

Then he asked how much money is in my 401(k). And my response was "sixteen dollars?" Again, how am I supposed to know? I barely even glance at my paycheck stubs. It's too fucking depressing, and every time I look at what I earned versus what the government lets me keep, I seriously consider trading my Obama liberal card for a Tea Party membership. So I just burn it. Fuck it. I don't have any idea how much of my paychecks I allocate into my "retirement plan" (LOL if you think I'm going to do anything other than DIE AT THIS JOB), and I could just walk into the other room and ask Jim, but who cares? All I know is that when my beer money runs low I have to fill out a "don't give a shit about being put in a shitty nursing home" form under his reproachful eye while asking if there's any way I can just deposit loose change or does it have to be actual whole dollars?

Dismayed, my hood accountant decided that I need to start paying attention to my money, at least a little bit. The first step involves documenting everything I spend for a month to see where the leaking cracks (or gaping holes and broken dams) might be. He thinks that once I have everything outlined in front of me I'll see where I've been pissing money away that could very well be put into some . . . um . . . what do white people call it? A savings account, I think? You got me. I've never heard of that shit before.

The one bright spot shining on my spendthrift ass is that I

don't have any credit card or student loan debt, because I never bothered to establish any fucking credit and I always pay for school out of my own pocket before deciding to waste my fucking money by dropping the hell out. SMART.

So I'm going to do it. I'm not making any commitments other than agreeing (1) not to alter my spending for the next four weeks, and (2) not lie about it. He's going to go through all my fucking bank statements anyway, so it's pretty fucking pointless. Here is the deal, in case you want to play along at home:

1. Write down everything you spend, every day. No purchase is too small; including newspapers, train fare, cab rides, *StreetWise*, WHATEVER.
2. Keep track of days you are working versus days you are off.
3. Save your receipts so you can itemize the purchases. No, you can't just write: "Target $120," you have to write exactly what you bought at Target, to figure out whether you really needed it.
4. Track your cash spending.
5. Suffer endless depression when you see what a disgusting spendthrift you are after in-depth critical analysis. Um, that might just be me. Anyway, you dudes should totally DO THIS WITH ME. Let's feel like irresponsible teenagers together!

I already fucked it up and forgot I was doing this until late this week, so I didn't save shit or write a damn thing down. But I sort of remember what I spent at the end of last week and over the weekend. And then I randomly wrote shit down here and there because, frankly, shit was getting a little embarrassing.

RANDOM

- CVS $120 (happy pills)
- Urban Outfitters $32 (age-inappropriate hat and gloves)
- Red Line Tap $14 (cover to see Vince's band + cheap beers)
- Sonny's $18 (lottery tickets, a jar of salsa, and two cans of Diet Coke)
- Lulu's $48 (dinner with Alexis. I paid.)
- Fresh flowers from Stems $27
- Lamp from Dania Furniture $39
- Magazine stand approx. $30 (*Elle, Spin, FADER, NYLON, URB, BUST*)
- Binny's $16 (2 four-packs of Allagash White)
- Ashley Stewart jumpsuit $35 (It's sexy.)

SUNDAY

- Evanston 1st $42 (bottle of Bulleit)
- 7-Eleven $6 (water and *Entertainment Weekly*)
- Kuma's $60 (Jamesons + burgers with Melissa)

TUESDAY

- Davis Pantry $9 (2 yogurts, Chex cereal, iced tea)
- Sprint $165 (phone bill)
- DIRECTV $62 (I cannot miss my shows.)

- Bally's $21 (gym membership. Pfffft.)
- Amazon $53 (Sony stereo headphones, *The Kids Are All Right* DVD, Maps & Atlases CD)
- ATM $40 (I owe Kate.)
- Transit card $20
- The Southern $64 (dinner and drinks with Amanda and Laura)
- C.O. Bigelow $42 (scented candles)
- Macy's $12 (umbrella to replace the one I left in a cab)
- Godiva $14 (truffles for me and a box for Amanda)
- Macy's $44 (Rachel Roy skull earrings that totally kick ass)

WEDNESDAY

- Trader Joe's $63
- Tickets to see Tapes 'n Tapes next weekend $30
- Best Buy $35 (*Inception* DVD, Greenhornes CD)
- The Cellar $0 (dinner with Tom—he paid!)

FRIDAY

- Starbucks $7
- Lunch tacos $6
- Amazon $17 (Kate's nail polish and the new Walkmen CD)
- Royal Canin calorie control $17 (stupid, fat Helen)
- Cocktails at Black Rock $22 (I think?)

SATURDAY

- Lady Gregory's $77 (brunch on me because I'm nice)
- Walgreens $13 (humidifier filter)
- Bath & Body Works online $23 (antibacterial soaps and shit)
- Between Scofflaw and Danny's and three different cabs $200+ (party time)

Let's stop here for the week, shall we? Especially since I am going to be off for the next four days and have nothing lined up except SHIT THAT COSTS MONEY. Holy fucking balls, friends. HOLY FUCKING BALLS. Eyeballing this list is mucho depressing, and keeping track of every little thing is exhausting. I'm not getting out my fancy calculator, because even at a goddamned glance I can tell I've spent easily eighteen billion motherfucking dollars in a week, LESS THAN A WEEK, and that is ridiculous. Good thing I plan on dying young and leaving whatever I have left to the cat colony I'm eventually going to start.

No rent paid (it's not time yet!) and no real groceries purchased. SMH. The only thing in my refrigerator is a bag of frozen raw shrimp, a seasoned mozzarella braid, and Crystal Light. But I have fresh flowers, balsam candles, lots of music, scratch-off lottery tickets, and SO MANY MAGAZINES to keep me company, so that makes it okay, right? I'd be embarrassed if it wasn't so awesome to stay liquored up and constantly entertained. SERIOUSLY. I buy books and music and magazines because Helen is boring and can't talk, and even though I have cable, sometimes there isn't a goddamned thing on TV. PLUS, how am I going to know this season's hottest lip gloss shades?! I can't be out here wearing coral while everyone else is wearing sparkling nudes! What I look like?!

I'm about to e-mail this to Jeff, even though I don't want to. I'm sure he's just going to go over it with a red marker, making slash marks over all my essentials. I can hear him now: "What do you need flowers for?" "Can't you just use bar soap?" NO, SIR, I CANNOT. Anyway, despite the fact that I am now suffering some crippling self-consciousness about my dumb-ass purchase history, I have another three weeks left of shaming my good sense. **401(ko'd)**.

skin rashes and arthritis

In the spring of 2005 my life totally fucking peaked. After years of sketchy rooming houses and terrible roommates, I finally had a decent-size living space that overlooked a terrifying alleyway strewn with needles and broken glass all to myself, and this little Honda that was basically patchworked together and just *shit* money. I had a handsome, successful boyfriend in medical school who could never be bothered to call me with any regularity or see me more than once a month. Living the goddamned dream, obviously. By this point I'd been working at an animal hospital for three years. Three years on the job is when you really start to find your fucking groove. You know everyone's crazy-making habits, you can rest relatively sure that your boss isn't going to fire you over something dumb, bitches stop "accidentally" microwaving your frozen meals in the break room at lunch, and you're finally comfortable enough to take a shit in the middle of the workday. So work was good. Real good. Like "push back from the table and unbutton your pants after a meal" good. Plus we had just gotten health insurance.

This boyfriend that I had? Kind of an asshole. But, in my twenty-five-year-old brain, if he could've just changed a couple of relatively harmless quirks (which bordered on pathological personality disorders), things were going to work out *perfectly* for the rest of my goddamned life. We had already been together a year, six months of which were kind of amazingly great for someone whose standards heretofore had required little more than "breathing," and then along came this man. This capital M-A-N who wore really fantastic Eddie Bauer sweaters and organized his bag by compartment rather than just throwing his shit in it like I did, and he had a bank account and a degree in chemistry from Northwestern and he'd hotly pursued me as if I was the most amazing person he had EVER MET IN HIS WHOLE LIFE until finally I succumbed and agreed to meet him at a record store to pretend like I had more than just a passing interest in house music while he shopped. I had never before felt so goddamned interesting. And this, mind you, was before all the joke writing and the performing and the bitches hugging me *so fucking hard* in the bathroom at the movie theater because of that one thing I wrote that one time about being depressed or something that meant *so very much* to them. Back then all I had was a manuscript: five hundred neatly typed pages of the novel I had spent the prior five years writing, and no one was trying to read that shit.

Good dates, decent conversations, sex that didn't make me want to jump off a fucking building. He didn't ask me to do anything gross or demoralizing in bed, and from what I could tell he wasn't harboring any secret wives or children or addictions or anything. We had been dating for a year and a half when, on a rare occasion in which he had spent an entire night in my actual bed, I woke up with a stomachache. And not an ordinary stomachache; it felt like there was an alien trapped under my skin, a hot, throbbing alien made of lava. And possibly a midsize Chevy sedan. I had never before felt pain as searing and horrible as what was coursing through my gut. I couldn't even zip my motherfucking jeans.

My jerk boyfriend wouldn't come with me to the hospital because he had big plans to jerk off and play video games, HATE MEN FOREVER DIE DIE BAD DIE BARF, so two hours later I lay in a sterile white bed totally alone with tubes in my arms and more tubes up my nose, signing a surgery consent form through vision-blurring fear tears because my bowel was obstructed and twisting on itself like a pretzel and if someone didn't fix that shit I was probably going to perforate my bowel and die. Just another Sunday, bro.

When my Crohn's comes roaring out of remission, due to stress or stress or goddamned motherfucking nerve-destroying *stress*, it makes me both tired and sad. AND BOSSY AND IRRITATED. And I know a lot of things suck, and so many people are going through so many terrible things, but to me, in this goddamned moment, nothing is worse than this gross-ass-shit disease. Yes, there are worse things, but since those things are not currently happening to *me*, this bullshit is the worst thing that has ever happened to anyone in the history of ever. It took seven months and a battery of tests for the doctors and nurses and radiologists to come up with a diagnosis, and as soon as they delivered it I was like, "Wouldn't euthanizing my ass be so much easier?"

I try not to ever talk about this business with strangers, because the word "disease" is off-putting and scary and I don't want anyone to ever move his or her chair away from me in public. But then that makes me feel all ashamed, like I'm hoarding some awful dirty secret. And lately I am trying to operate from a shame-free place. I'm trying not to fuck dudes I am too embarrassed to tell my friends about; I'm trying not to indulge my shameful habits as often as I used to, because burying shit at the bottom of the garbage is tiresome and boring; and so I am writing in this book that I have Crohn's disease, and its little bastard cousin ulcerative colitis, and twenty minutes ago I took a soupy shit that splattered all over the inside of my jeans because this complicated belt is obviously here to ruin my life. There, I said it. I have some horrible butt disease that you would never ever want to deal with, and I, er, *embrace* it. If you are my friend or my new hot piece or my old bitter enemy you will eventually find this shit out anyway, so I'd be a motherfucking idiot to try to hide it. Because eventually I will ruin your movie or your breakfast or your football game or your cousin's wedding or your graduation or your party or your concert or your REM sleep cycle with my poorly understood immunodeficiency inflammatory bowel disease.

That's right, my dude! She and I will rear our ugly heads when you least expect it and are least prepared to handle the, um, fallout . . . ? Like when you take us on that long road trip you've been talking about, and she and I ask you seven times to find us a truck stop because you couldn't find me something devoid of taste, texture, and nutrients to eat and I had no idea a sesame bagel would race through my guts like a goddamned greyhound. Or maybe you'll meet my special friend in the middle of that movie you really, *really* wanted to see and waited in line for three hours to get tickets for. And if you don't automatically want to leave at the sight of my sweaty forehead and panic face, you will after I've gone and come back fourteen fucking times. I have left *dozens* of plays and ceremonies and services and games and parties and events, and I have stayed home from ten times as many because my stupid stomach hurt and I had fucking diarrhea.

Crohn's disease is an inflammatory bowel disease that causes inflammation of the lining of the digestive tract. It can affect any part of the digestive tract, from the mouth to the anus, but is particularly fond of the small intestine. At least mine is, and she is located in my ileum, the end piece of my small intestine that connects it to my large one. Potential side effects: bone loss, eye problems, back pain, arthritis, liver swelling, gallstones, and skin problems. My joints hurt. And my gnarly skin is disgusting. Can't wait until my eyes fall out of their sockets and my bones shatter every time a strong wind blows.

So Crohn's is an immunodeficiency disease, which means that the cells in my body that are supposed to protect against infection don't recognize food and the normal, harmless bacteria that are in my intestine. Let's break it down this way: An innocuous piece of bread is trying to make its way from my mouth to my booty hole. And it's pretty smooth cilia sailing, but only until the second it hits these grody old guts. My receptor cells, which should be like, "Oh, hello, food! What's up, delicious nutrients?" instead are all, "INTRUDER!" and flood my intestines with little soldiering white blood cells armed to the teeth to fight off the enemy. And while they are entrenched in battle, swords and spears and bayonets aloft, I am in a ridiculous amount of pain (like childbirth pain, real talk), which is typically followed by a torrent of bloody shit (and much humiliated apologizing to whomever I happen to be hanging out with at the time). YEARS of this gnarly infighting (think Capulets and Montagues, Israel and Palestine, Biggie and Tupac) have left my intestines a veritable wasteland of scar tissue. Picture the circumference of your average drinking straw. Now imagine shoving a chicken breast through it. (To be fair, a chewed-up chicken breast, but I think you get what I'm saying.) There are parts of my intestines that are so thick with useless scar tissue that whatever I eat has just that teeny tiny passageway to squeak through. And with all that tussling and fighting going on around it, food rarely survives the journey intact. It just liquefies itself into runny chocolate pudding (on a good day) or smelly brown pee (on a bad one).

I have almost reached my lifetime limit of radiation exposure, as I have had three colonoscopies, seven CT scans, two barium series (small bowel imaging), and a capsule endoscopy (I swallowed a camera in a capsule that took digital pictures of my entire intestinal tract as it moved through my system until I shit it out). I have had the contents of my stomach sucked out through my nose. I have shit in a bucket every day for two weeks and collected samples and shipped them FedEx to a lab. I've had various sections of my bowel collected and biopsied. I have had to vomit while a doctor dude sat and watched and took notes, and I don't mean in a sex-fetish way. My ass was hanging out the back of a too-small gown and everything. Awful.

My GI doctor is supermodel hot, totally fucking smoking, oh my lord, handsome as a motherfucker, and it pains me to imagine the ridiculous joke your cruel god is playing on my life; watching me and laughing his ass off while a Michelangelo sculpture tells me to relax my asshole so he can stick first his fingers, and then the scope, into it. The first time he asked me about "the consistency of my last stool" I almost left my pants behind and ran screaming out the door to get a cab home. It's the very worst kind of humiliation really, curled up on a cold table naked from the waist down lying fetus-style while a man hotter than any man you could ever imagine getting busy with spreads your butt cheeks and examines the skin around your hairy asshole. And he tries to be normal and talk to you about normal shit ("Where do you work?" "What's your favorite band?" "What do you do for fun?") while he lubes up those dexterous digits so he can palpate your colon. Try being comfortable during that! This is a dude I would be weirded out and nervous talking to while fully clothed and standing at the bus stop, let alone when his face is six inches from the crack of my *ass*. I wish you could've seen my face the time I shit on him a little bit during an exam. There are no words.

I spent my entire childhood with the ghetto diagnosis of "weak stomach." You know what the fuck I mean, when black people let your little black ass shit her pants at school but still don't drag you to a doctor because it's easier to pretend that you just ate too much dinner. I spent half my junior year in high school in the second-floor bathroom of Beardsley Hall, the one tucked in the back where the school hid all the ESL kids and that had the least trafficky bathroom. I was always sitting in there, crammed into a stall at the end, doing my chemistry homework and burning up my asshole.

So think about the last time you had horrible diarrhea. I mean, use your mind grapes and *really* get back in that place. That hot, flushed, desperate, churning, panicky, butt-clenchy place. CONCENTRATE. Okay, are you there yet? What about now? Are you afraid you might crap yourself? Or that the bathroom is too far for you to make it in time? That this heavy, immobile, butts-to-nuts traffic won't let up before you get to an exit? That someone will walk in the bathroom, recognize your shoes, then go running back to class to tell everyone what they caught you doing? That the train is going *backward* because the motherfucker is moving so slow? That your first day on your new job might have gone a whole lot better if you hadn't spent your lunch break in the bathroom across the street at Nordstrom because you don't really know these people very well yet? That your new boyfriend will be totally grossed out because it's your third date and you shouldn't have gotten the flaming cheese and now you're back at his apartment and are forced to ruin the mood (IN HIS TINY STUDIO) with a big, noisy, smelly, obnoxious shit so you turn on the faucet in the bathtub because it's louder than the sink and you hope like hell he was drunk enough to pass out and doesn't notice you flushing his toilet thirteen goddamned times?

Welcome to my universe, love. Where I do not get to be lovely and delicate and demure because sooner rather than later I am going to have to talk to you about shit. When this bullshit is out of remission my life is a *literal* shitshow, on every channel. Imagine the worst diarrhea you've ever had, and imagine having that shit every single day. You could light a match on my poor rectum some days, I swear to God. I am the only child-free ass-hole on the planet with a tube of Desitin in her purse. And in the bathroom. And in the nightstand. And let's be for real. I have a sense of humor about everything, this included.

I was finally diagnosed almost eight years ago, and at the time I was GODDAMNED MORTIFIED. While I was happy to have an answer, I was pretty fucking bummed to have some chronic, permanent shit at age twenty-five. I don't have the genetics required to live to super old age (don't cry for me, I've come to terms with it), but the prospect of even forty years dragging along with this bullshit was a lot to, um, stomach.

There is no cure, which is totally fucking awesome. I'd take syphilis over this shit because at least then I could get a shot in my vag and be right back on the horse a week later. In addition to no cure there is also no known cause, which makes climbing my disconnected family tree to inspect every branch for digestive difficulty *even more* awesome! My mom had MS; my dad was a vicious drunk with a heart problem; one of my sisters had cancer, while another has had a couple of heart episodes—where the fuck did *this shit* come from? I'm supposed to only have a predisposition for gorgeous skin and a fat ass, both of which I got already. (Thanks, parents!) This stomach shit is supposed to be in someone else's fucking family.

I take eight horse pills a day and massive amounts of steroids when I'm not feeling good. My list of noes is longer than the credits of the last good movie you've seen and includes, but is certainly not limited to: sugar, caffeine, raw fruits and vegetables, alcohol, sweets, grease, cereal, dairy, yeast, beef, pork, chocolate, spice, flavor, variety, and deliciousness. Which is basically impossible to adhere to and totally the reason I occasionally come frighteningly close to shitting myself on the bus. Sometimes I gotta pretend to be normal, even if it means I have to wear a diaper to book club. I can't order rice and boiled chicken at every restaurant, especially ones that don't have a children's menu. (All praises be to the delightfully bland children's menu.) Food is absolutely fucking delicious. I should've called my blog *bitches gotta shit.*

the tapeworm diet

It's hilarious to me when people try to pretend not to know why they are fat. Like, really, dude? You eat three small meals and exercise an hour every day, yet somehow have no idea why there is a spare tire around your waist? Because if those things were true you would be skinny. Skinny-er. Skinny-ish. Does each of those three meals consist of Big Macs washed down with an entire ham? By "exercise" do you mean "stand up"? I have never in my life pretended to have some undiagnosed "glandular problem" or speculated about a goddamned "slow metabolism." I eat bad things and then go to sleep immediately afterward. There, I solved the mystery of fatness for you. You're welcome. So here is why I am a massive, gigantic person:

1. My delicious, delicious feelings. I was never taught how to cope with the batshit voices rattling around in my head. Talking about my kid problems wasn't necessarily frowned upon, but it definitely wasn't encouraged. But we always had comforting Little Debbies in the house. Nutty Bars, Oatmeal Pies, all that delicious dollar-store shit. And when I had a, um, *challenging* day at school I would come home and grab a Star Crunch or a Raisin Creme Pie and by "a" I mean "several." Then I'd build an impenetrable snack fort and read *Beezus and Ramona* then take a predinner nap, and when I woke up, everything would be magically better. Food is love, and I was married to cookies. Our family did (or didn't do) all the things that make you fat: never having dinner around the dining room table, eating right before bed, Kool-Aid in the refrigerator . . . you get it. I was a chubby little poor kid who ate a lot of snack cakes because boys thought I was ugly. Not to mention the fact that my parents were tired and old and the only pigskins we tossed around were the ones my father had liberally sprinkled with black pepper and hot sauce. Mmm, crunchy.

2. The vegetables I had to finish before I could leave the table always came from a can. And if they hadn't, they'd been cooked with a pig's foot or a slab of bacon floating in the water or some other unhealthy shit and leached of any nutritional value whatsoever after the third hour of lard-added boiling. I'm not telling you anything new when I say that poor people don't buy a whole lot of fresh vegetables, particularly when they are poor people

with young, wasteful children. We ate a lot of Hamburger Helper. A lot of Rice-A-Roni, the San Francisco treat. Shake 'N Bake. All the foods that had commercials. All that delicious high-sodium shit. Cup Noodles, Lipton Rice & Sauce, you could get cases of them shits for hella cheap. Celebratory dinners at Pizza Hut. Sunday mornings after church at Old Country Buffet. I liked frozen corn and canned peas and probably didn't have a tomato that hadn't been fried or wasn't glistening atop a double cheeseburger until I was a goddamned teenager.

3. If you've never been skinny, the appeal of thinness < the tastiness of simple carbohydrates. There's freedom in a double-digit elastic waistband. It's like, what's a handful of Milk Duds if you're already fat? Who cares whether this Coke is diet if you're already at the far end of the BMI? Get in me, movie theater popcorn! I ALREADY HAVE A DOUBLE FUCKING CHIN. Yes, I will have another beer! Of course I'm going to finish what's left on my plate! I'm already wearing maternity yoga pants; let's see how far these bitches stretch!

I need to lose some weight, though. Everybody and their mother is always taking goddamned pictures of my motherfucking skin beard, and the Internet is already full of my unflattering fatness, plus you assholes keep recognizing me while I'm waiting outside Longman & Eagle for Sunday brunch, and I *really* want you to walk away thinking, "OMG, she's totes pretty in real life and her moles are super understated and classy instead of gross." I really do. I spent half an hour on the elliptical yesterday, and I did the chest press until it felt like my rib cage was going to explode through my tits, but I also had four bites of macaroni and cheese with bacon in it. Maybe five. OKAY, SIX. I have to get my shit together, friends. BUT HOW?! *welp*

THE TWINKIE DIET

A typical day in the life of Kansas State University nutrition researcher Mark Haub, creator of the Junk Food Diet, which consists of 60 percent junk food supplemented by a protein shake, multivitamin pills, and a can of green beans or four stalks of celery every day. He avoided meat, whole grains, and fruits. September 10, 2010: A double espresso; two servings of Hostess Twinkies; one Centrum Advance pill; one serving of Little Debbie Star Crunch cookies (my jam!); a Diet Mountain Dew (barf); half a serving of Doritos Cool Ranch corn chips; two servings of Kellogg's Corn Pops cereal; a serving of whole milk (squirt!); half a serving of raw baby carrots; one-and-a-half servings of Duncan Hines family-style chewy fudge brownie; half a serving of Little Debbie Zebra Cake; one serving of Muscle Milk protein shake drink; total: 1,589 calories.

Just reading that shit makes my fucking teeth hurt. I think I also might've just caught diabetes through the computer screen. This can't be life, right? Snack cakes and baby carrots? NO, IT CANNOT.

NUTRISYSTEM

The theory: Losing weight is easier if you outsource meal-management chores. Nutrisystem determines portions, prepares and delivers your meals, and tells you what to eat and when. Guaranteed calorie restriction, the tried-and-true weight-loss tactic. The cost: Meal plans range from $250 to $500 a month.

In theory: This shit sounds fucking perfect. I spend $500 a month because I have to have the jammiest package with the sickest perks, of course, and in return I am shipped delicious, calorie-conscious meals that basically do all the work for my lazy, slovenly ass. What could go wrong?

The *actual* cost: $500 + whatever I already spend on food per month as it is, because I know better than to think that I will be happy and full carrying around freeze-dried celery meals and fat-free pudding desserts. It's like when I used to have a Lean Cuisine appetizer prior to my Lean Cuisine main course. Double the money, still fat.

THE TAPEWORM DIET

So this is a real thing. It's illegal in America, because we hate infectious parasites, but other people in countries that understand how hard it is for a bitch to keep her grubby little mitts off cheese dogs obviously have governments that care about them. These fucking fascists. I WANT MY SUCCUBUS. Okay, so the idea is that introducing a tapeworm into the body means that the food you eat is split between your own body and that of the tapeworm. You are a host, and the tapeworm uses you by attaching suckers to your stomach and feeding on the foods that you eat. The tapeworm is an additional means of reducing the amount of calories that you absorb WITHOUT reducing the calories that you consume. The traditional way of becoming infected with a tapeworm is by eating raw meat or by coming into contact with infected feces and/or other foods containing tapeworms. However, for the purposes of dieting, methods would include the tablet form.

Sounds amazing. Worm-infected meat. Totally not gonna die.

THE GRAPEFRUIT DIET

The twelve-day grapefruit diet menu:

Breakfast: 8 ounces of unsweetened juice or one half grapefruit, two eggs, and two slices of bacon.

Lunch: 8 ounces of unsweetened juice or one half grapefruit, a salad with low-fat dressing, and one meat entrée cooked in any style. You can double or even triple your portions if you want. (This speaks to me.)

Dinner: 8 ounces of unsweetened juice or one half grapefruit, a salad with low-fat dressing, one red or green vegetable (cooked in butter with spices if you are feeling like a fucking badass), and any meat or fish, cooked in any style. You can double or triple your entrée!!!

Bedtime snack: 8 ounces of tomato juice or skim milk. (Recipe for a nightmare, blech.) You also must drink eight 8-ounce glasses of water over the course of the day.

I hate grapefruits. Ever since I was a kid. I just can't handle that bitterness, the way my salivary glands go apeshit at the mere mention of them. I'm frothing at the mouth right now just typing this shit. Impossible. Next.

SLIMFAST

Your 1,200 calories a day will come from three snacks (half a banana, a pear, or a SlimFast snack bar, for example), two SlimFast meal replacements (a bar or a shake), and one 500-calorie meal you prepare. SlimFast is best for people who need to lose about twenty pounds, which should take eight to ten weeks.

My sister did SlimFast once and her farts were bad enough to singe my fucking nose hairs. She burned a hole through the seat of her jeans. Not even kidding. We had to keep a fire extinguisher next to the goddamned toilet. I know you think I'm making this up but there was literal fire shooting out of her butt! It was like living with a dragon. A skinny-fat, cranky dragon that could light the dinner candles with her asshole.

THE BABY-FOOD DIET

A celebrity-fad diet that reportedly involves replacing breakfast and lunch with about fourteen jars of baby food (about twenty-five to seventy-five calories each) and then eating a sensible dinner.

I want to see you bitches walking around with jars of turkey dinner or mango banana peas clinking around inside your expensive handbags. I want to see you on park benches in the middle of the day daintily eating puréed carrots and beets from those teeny little spoons because nothing else will fit into those teeny little jars. I would die happy. And until Gerber makes carne asada tacos in portable, baby-proof packaging, I'ma just leave this one right here.

BEING A VEGAN

In January I read this article in *The New York Times* called "How to Go Vegan" about how Bill Clinton's decision to adopt a vegan lifestyle totally convinced the writer to try it out herself and almost even made me want to try that shit. A vegan is someone who, for various reasons, usually batshit craziness (just kidding, lolololol), chooses to avoid using or consuming animal products. While vegetarians choose not to consume flesh foods, vegans also avoid dairy and eggs, as well as fur, leather, wool, down, and cosmetics or chemical products tested on animals.

I'm too poor and it's too much fucking work. There, I said it. I really wish I was the type of person who owned a Prius and didn't work fifty hours a week and could spend time in the grocery store reading labels to make sure that there isn't a drop of gelatin or honey in every single thing I put in my cart at Whole Foods. And yes, that's an excuse but also yes, I JUST CAN'T. I can hardly see straight at the end of the day, and it takes every ounce of the little strength I have left not to make an entire nutritious meal out of the samples scattered around the fucking store.

THE CIGARETTE DIET

Popular in the 1920s. At the time, Lucky Strike cigarette company wanted to boost sales, so they used the appetite-curbing nature of nicotine to their advantage. With the ad campaign slogan "Reach for a Lucky instead of a sweet," Lucky Strike enticed a lot of ladies to smoke rather than consume extra calories. And the campaign worked: sales were boosted more than 200 percent in the 1920s with the use of that slogan. Other tobacco companies jumped on the bandwagon during this time period and promoted smoking as a weight-loss method.

Skinny and dead from lung cancer. This is not the move.

THE SLEEPING BEAUTY DIET

Elvis Presley tried this hilarious diet right around the time he had trouble fitting into his trademark 1970s jumpsuits. The belief behind it: if you were heavily sedated for several days, you'd "sleep off" the weight and wake up thinner.

A dream. A *literal* dream come true. If life was fair and karma was real I would have an IV in my arm and a spandex jumpsuit on my ass, while floating on a bliss cloud made of Dilaudid and Propofol. This is probably a sign of some deep-seated depression, and I probably shouldn't admit this publicly, but all I ever want to goddamned do is sleep. I want to sleep, watch wrestling on Hulu on my phone, and eat refined sugar and simple carbohydrates. I'm not allowed to, because life is a cruel mistress, but if I had my way I would get up every couple of days for a taco refuel and lapse right back into my medicated diet coma. The only downside is that you'd have to be a goddamned millionaire to pull this shit off. So unless I hit the lottery or learn how to sneer while swiveling my hips and playing the guitar, this one might be just beyond my reach. That said, I'm going to the corner store to get some scratch-off tickets. A girl can dream, can't she?

EATING ONLY RAW FOODS

NOT THE SAME AS VEGANISM, BRO. Man, who knew?!

Raw foodies don't cook their dinner, and while I'm sure that preserves all the vitamins and healthy shit, all I can think of is that episode of *Sex and the City* when the girls ate at that raw restaurant and Miranda said the chunky green soup tasted like "lawn in a bowl" before eating half a goddamned pizza on the walk home. Okay, so here's what the diet looks like: Raw fish such as sashimi, ceviche, or cold-smoked or cured fish. Raw cheese such as goat or sheep. Raw nuts and seeds, raw and dried fruit, raw and dried veggies, raw soups like gazpacho and cucumber, and raw meats such as steak tartare and filet americain. Also cold-smoked or cured meats. Sprouted breads, bagels, and tortilla wraps. Plus raw cakes, ice creams, smoothies, alcoholic drinks, juices, cookies, and snacks.

Hot food is just better. That is my childish answer and I'm sticking with it. Food should be hot, Goldilocks. Most food should be hot. I'm into this ice cream and alcohol business, though. Raw ice cream could be my new jam.

THE COTTON BALL DIET

You replace meals or snacks with cotton balls soaked in gelatin, or just dry cotton balls. In other versions of the diet you eat the cotton balls before meals, and they prevent you from eating too much. The rationale is that the cotton balls contain some calories, and they fill you up, preventing you from wanting to eat anything fattening, like real food. STOP IT.

THE CABBAGE SOUP DIET

The cabbage soup diet is a radical weight-loss diet designed around the heavy consumption of a low-calorie cabbage soup over the course of seven days.

Day 1: Cabbage soup plus as much fruit as desired, excluding bananas. SHIT ALL MOTHERFUCKING DAY.

Day 2: Cabbage soup plus vegetables, including 1 jacket (baked) potato with a little butter. SHIT ALL MOTHER-FUCKING DAY.

Day 3: Cabbage soup plus fruit and vegetables, excluding potatoes and bananas. SHIT ALL MOTHERFUCKING DAY.

Day 4: Cabbage soup plus up to eight bananas and as much skim milk as desired. SHIT ALL MOTHERFUCKING DAY.

Day 5: Cabbage soup plus up to 10 ounces (283 grams) of beef and up to six tomatoes. SHIT ALL MOTHER-FUCKING DAY.

Day 6: Cabbage soup plus as much beef and vegetables (excluding potatoes) as desired. SHIT ALL MOTHER-FUCKING DAY.

Day 7: Cabbage soup plus brown rice, vegetables (excluding potatoes), and unsweetened fruit juice. SHIT ALL MOTHERFUCKING DAY.

Day 8: DIE FROM DEHYDRATION, but ten pounds lighter, OMG, your shriveled little dried-up corpse looks AMAZE.

THE BLOOD-TYPE DIET

The Eat Right for Your Blood Type diet encourages people to eat certain foods and avoid others based on their blood type. What you can eat and how you are supposed to exercise on this diet depends on who you are.

If you're blood type O (as in "old," humanity's oldest bloodline) your digestive tract retains the memory of ancient times (WHAT?!), so your metabolism will benefit from lean meats, poultry, and fish. You're supposed to restrict grains, breads, and legumes and to enjoy vigorous exercise.

Type A (for "agrarian") does best on a vegetarian diet, "the inheritance of their more settled and less-warlike farmer ancestors," according to the dude who wrote the book. The type A diet is made up of soy proteins, grains, and organic vegetables and encourages gentle exercise.

The nomadic blood type B has a tolerant digestive system and can enjoy low-fat dairy, meat, and produce but, among other things, should avoid wheat, corn, and lentils. If you're type B, it's recommended you exercise moderately.

The "modern" blood type AB has a sensitive digestive tract and should avoid chicken, beef, and pork but enjoy seafood, tofu, dairy, and most produce. The fitness regimen for ABs is calming exercises.

How do I find out what my blood type is? I've been in the hospital a hundred times and have had my blood drawn three times that amount, so how come I have no idea what the hell it is? I was too busy sleeping in high school to sell platelets, and now, when I go donate blood, one glance at my medical chart and they're all, "Yeah, right, sick person. I'd rather take my chances with that heroin addict over there." Seriously. The organ-donor box on the back of my driver's license reads, "ARE YOU FUCKING KIDDING ME?" I'm just going to call myself an AB because shrimp is delicious and I refuse to live without soft, stinky cheese. And calming exercises sound hella wonderful. I can chant soothingly with my eyes closed while in child's pose. Let's do this.

BRIDAL BOOTCAMP

The woman who came up with this business researched the boot camp training methods of the US military and adapted them for cranky, stressed-out, sleep-deprived women teetering on the brink of sanity. She promises that her program will help pissed-off brides-to-be build muscle, shape up, burn fat, and put them on the path toward leading a healthy lifestyle. The program includes six-month, three-month, and four-week regimens, depending on how much time you have until your wedding date. Each regimen includes a specific diet, fitness program, supplement advice, and other information. Every bridezilla starts out on level one, which involves an hour of military-style training four times a week. Great, exactly what you need after fighting with your bitch mom for three hours about lilac napkins and less-expensive place settings.

If I ever get married I am going to wear pants. Loose-fitting, flowing palazzo pants that don't bunch up in the crotch, specially made according to my measurements and affixed with some sort of adjustable waistband to account for any calzones or half-priced Easter candy I might consume between the time that I have them made and the time I finally make it to the courthouse. I will not be doing any bridal boot camps that will only result in my having unrealistically beautiful wedding pictures that will mock me and my failing marriage until my husband inevitably leaves me and my cottage cheese thighs to our own devices.

Don't try any of this crazy fucking shit. I'm going to scrape the icy freezer burn off this pint of Ben & Jerry's Peanut Butter World (that shit is banging, yo) and finish this leftover pasta salad, and then I'm going to pack Healthy Choice meals that I get on sale at Target in my lunch and order my cheeseburgers without the bun at restaurants. And instead of going to the gym twice a week I will try to go four times, maybe five if there's nothing good on TV. I just tossed out all my full-fat salad dressings and gave the college boys across the hall my emergency frozen burritos. Tomorrow I might even take the stairs. Baby steps. And safer than a goddamned tapeworm, HOLY SHIT.

i want to put a fat bitch
on network television

My writing partner, Ian Belknap, and I wrote a badass imaginary television show. If I ran the world you'd be watching this on a premium network right now.

The Irby and Ian Project (IIP) centers on Nell, the host of a popular Internet radio show, *Nell in a Handbasket,* where she gives brash, bracingly honest, bawdy but wise relationship advice. Nell's on-mic command and poise is countered by the uncertainty and chaos of her personal life. Like many of her generation, Nell attempts (and mostly fails) to navigate the mind-crushingly horrible gut punch that is modern dating. The IIP also explores the way relationships morph and decay and people's lives change (marriage, babies, property taxes, parents in elder care, etc.), the friction that can rise between friends who have money and those who don't, and navigating the minefield of interracial dating and friendship.

Though a bright and self-educated woman, Nell cannot take her own advice. Assured and never at a loss on her show, in her real life, too often Nell feels the sting of getting left behind by those around her, who seem to have gotten a manual for living that she never received. She barely feels like an adult; her peers are running laps around her on the track of life.

Nell is at the center of a group of friends who have surpassed her in the ways that matter: romantic, financial, familial, and having a sense of purpose. Nell's caught in the trap of being smart enough to be pissed about all the societal pressure to find happiness through a mate and money, and bighearted enough to yearn for real love and companionship in her life. She's caught between believing she deserves a life mate and believing it's a complete impossibility; between believing prosperity and fulfillment are attainable and her dim economic prospects. She's been burned many times before but is too resilient and/or deluded to abandon hope entirely. She's totally the kind of person you root for.

CHARACTERS

Nell
African-American, pretty face, heavy, thirties, host of
Nell in a Handbasket, *so named for the MAJESTIC AND INIMITABLE NELL CARTER.*
A bit of an asshole, albeit in an endearing way. She is not a mean person, just somebody who doesn't suffer fools gladly. She

vacillates between being a misanthropic loner and being totally charming and personable. Nell is a badass, but secretly sort of miserable and displaced. While hosting her show, Nell is warm, reassuring, attentive, and wise. Hers is exactly the voice you hope to hear when you call the suicide hotline. Off-mic, Nell is harsh, sharp-tongued, and surly. Wherever she goes, Nell is the most quick-witted person in the room, so she spends most of her time gritting her teeth and rolling her eyes at the pageant of dumb-assery that surrounds her. She's a truth-teller who will give you a decisive smackdown when you deserve it.

Though Nell is a towering and authentic force of nature, she is insecure about her looks, her body. Everything about her physical self that the beauty industry and media have told her all her life is wrong. The latest indignity: Nell just got dumped for being "too smart" by a dude who works at Foot Locker, a dude she'd concluded was a prospectless loser. This is just another in a long string of dead-end relationships that heightens her mistrust and pushes her to make progressively dumber choices in men. It's a parade of idiots and scumbags.

Nell hosts her show in her tiny, dingy, depressing apartment, dispensing sound and no-nonsense relationship advice. This radio gig pays no money to speak of but requires a huge investment of her time and energy, so Nell's is a marginal life. She's forced to take a series of hilarious and demeaning and stupid jobs for beer money: landscaping, cater-waitering, painting houses, moving, bike messengering, housecleaning, dog walking, pedicab driving, etc. She changes jobs constantly, because she quits the second she's irritated, which is always. She's broke all the time, always relying on money from friends, and in particular her brother, Jerrell, which causes enduring friction.

Despite her dark moods, her stubborn poverty, and her temper, Nell maintains a mostly positive attitude. Her dating life is absolute garbage, but she continues to try to bag sketchy dudes she meets in dive bars and on the Internet. She keeps trying, if for no other reason than the sake of her listeners. (She feels an obligation to them to "stay in the game" and to accumulate interesting—or merely cautionary—tales to tell.) Nell jumps on every dating trend, partly to report back on them on her show, and partly because she secretly hopes one of them will pay off—speed dating, blind dates, Craigslist weirdos, well-intentioned matchmaking friends—and all of which ultimately culminate in absurd and awkward non-matches.

Nell's a generous and valued friend and has a wealth of "people" knowledge, which makes her exceptional at doling out advice. Her people knowledge ends abruptly at herself, though, so she's kind of a mess.

Dan
Caucasian, forties, pale, haggard, peeved.
The computer nerd/IT guy who produces the radio show; he's the behind-the-scenes guy who keeps it running. White, caustic, and a malcontent and cantankerous bastard. He's grossly overqualified for this pissant job but hasn't been able to find anything better since he got downsized from a Fortune 500 company three years back. He's bitter about working for this scattered idiot, though inwardly, he MIGHT concede Nell is quite good at fielding questions from listeners and synthesizing her own experience into helpful stories, but in all other respects is a chaotic wreck. If you put a gun to his head, he might say Nell's a star who, if she got out of her own goddamn way a little bit, could be wildly successful.

Dan has much that Nell thinks she wants: a marriage that's

not hopelessly acrimonious or dysfunctional, two healthy kids, a house he's been (barely) able to hang on to during the downturn, but he's constantly overwhelmed by the demands of it all. (Think: Pete Hornberger from *30 Rock*.) He's constantly reminding Nell: "Cherish your freedom; I'm on house arrest till these little jerkwads move out." He loves his family but is burnt out. He pines for nothing more than silence and inactivity. He lusts less after the sexual encounters Nell has (though he does that, too) than her freedom. Dan and Nell have an adversarial dynamic; when off-mic, they one-up each other with lacerating wit. Their common ground: a near-constant exasperation with other people and grudging respect for each other's skills and smarts. They are bound by mutual need: her show would never fly without him, and he'd be up shit creek without this job that's beneath him. Nell secretly respects Dan's monogamy and curmudgeonly-but-loving parenting; Dan secretly respects how principled and bullshit-free Nell is and the courage he knows it takes to follow your own path.

Jerrell
African-American, late twenties, fit, prosperous, sexy.
Nell's younger brother is her polar opposite: crisp, put together, ambitious, focused, and responsible. He did everything he was supposed to—scholarship, internships, career—and their parents (along with society) have rewarded him greatly. Nell resents him but she desperately needs his sporadic financial intervention to bail her out of jams, so she tries to get along with him in her bristly way. He has moved back to town after an absence of several years to take a promotion and is a little shocked to discover her lack of progress: she hasn't finished college or

started a family; she can't hold a job and is always borrowing money she can't pay back. Jerrell is baffled by his sister's attachment to her radio show, since Jerrell has a hard time separating Nell from the lonesome losers who call seeking her counsel. He decides to make Nell his latest project, to make it his mission to "life coach" her through her many difficulties and ensure that she becomes the kind of success he wants her to be. Jerrell is an overbearing pain in the ass, but he wants what's best for Nell, and she knows it, so she tolerates him. And his money.

Calvin

African-American, thirties, good-looking, rich.

A banker who tossed Nell in the "friend zone" immediately after meeting her. Nell never got over it, has been sweet on him ever since, and continues to hang out with him in hopes that one day they will have hammered, regret-it-right-away sex or something. He sees her as the sister he never had. (The least sexy thing a man could think about a woman.) He turns to Nell for advice on his love life, which is agony for her, considering he dates only soulless third-tier models with vacant eyes and empty skulls. Calvin's the kind of guy who will buy dinner for everyone in the restaurant because he can and because he's the kind of dude whose main objective is to keep the party going. Fun, kind of fratty, and way superficial—designer suits, expensive shoes, and pricey sports cars. He's obsessed with the surface, consumed with outward appearances, and unable or unwilling to develop lasting or meaningful relationships. His friendship with Nell is the most real thing in his life, but you can sense that below the surface he's just using her to up his game with women. He is also the champion of most of her bad choices, encouraging her to keep putting herself out there with men, even if the results could be detrimental to her rapidly deteriorating self-esteem.

Gail and Andy
Caucasian, thirties, slim, vital, productive, appealing, based on my good friends Jess and Rodney.

Nell's best friends; a contented, energetic couple who are "doing everything right." They met young, fell hopelessly and permanently in love, got married, are still totally crazy about each other, and are expecting their first baby. Their house is perfect: warm, relaxed, inviting, always full of people—a stark contrast to the squalor of Nell's living space and studio. Nell spends most of her free time there, being fed and coddled while she complains about her sex life, etc. Nell hates to admit it, but she envies them. She's also apprehensive about the changes to the current dynamic their new baby will bring. Gail and Andy throw weekly dinner parties to which Nell has a standing invitation; she's always bringing the wrong cheap wine, and her friends are too gracious not to drink it. Needless to say, Dan cannot stand these people.

Vanessa and Gretchen
Nell's two good ladyfriends.

Also unlucky in love, they are Nell's close confidantes and fellow soldiers in the war against sleeping alone each night. Former high school rivals, they only tolerate each other because of Nell. They are in constant competition, both for men and for the lion's share of Nell's friendship.

Vanessa
Caucasian, thirties, slutty redhead.
A super-fun, morally bankrupt party girl who sleeps with random strangers without ever holding down a real job. Vanessa is happy sport-banging dudes for fun and not giving much thought to the future.

Gretchen
Caucasian, thirties, bossy, judgmental.
Bitter, perpetually single, borderline spinster who wishes desperately she weren't. Gretchen is engaged in a constantly escalating search to find a husband. She's obsessed with trying to find a mate and have children, but she's crabby and negative and controlling, so men run from her.

Nell relies on each of them for different things: Vanessa is there for sexy girl talk and bird-dogging dudes, and Gretchen is always there to bitch about how horrible men are and to go shopping with for sensible shoes.

PILOT

Pouring rain on a beautiful, tree-lined street in an affluent neighborhood. Parked along either side of the street are sleek luxury cars. Giggling teenage girls run by while trying to shield themselves with a single umbrella. A good-looking man in a sharp suit walks an immaculately groomed poodle while holding a folded newspaper over his head. All of a sudden you hear a thunderous boom, then another, and a small car comes chugging and rattling down the street, grumbling at a deafening volume. It pulls to a stop in front of one of the houses, smoke billowing from under the hood, and after a few seconds the passenger door bangs open.

Nell, dressed in sparkly party clothes and hooker shoes, emerges from the passenger side after squeezing herself out from under the wheel and climbing across the front seat. She opens the back door, which swings precariously on its hinges, and removes a red insulated pizza delivery bag. She balances the pizza on the roof of the car, wrestles with the door to get it closed, and then takes a second to pull her dress from where it has gotten stuck, bunched into the top of her tights. She has a hard time walking up to the front door of the house, teetering and stumbling in her dangerously high heels. After carefully climbing the steps, Nell is just about to ring the doorbell when her cell phone starts ringing. You can see her briefly agonizing over whether she should answer the phone while technically at work and standing in the rain, but she goes for it.

She balances the pizza in one arm while trying to remove the phone from her bra and nearly drops them both a couple of times before she finally gets the phone to her ear. She answers the phone and stands there listening for a good ten seconds, shoulders slumped, clothes getting soaked through. The door inside the house flies open, and on the other side of the glass door stands a middle-aged white man in sweatpants and a T-shirt that totally doesn't fit in with the surrounding neighborhood. He looks really pissed off. He opens his mouth to say something to Nell, but she holds up a finger to shush him, and he responds by sighing angrily and looking at his watch. She says to the person on the phone, "How the fuck can YOU break up with ME? You work at fucking Foot Locker!" She slams the phone shut and pulls the pizza box from its protective carrier and tells the owner of the house what he owes her. He pointedly looks at his watch again and puts his wallet away. "Thirty-one minutes," he says smugly. "That pizza is free."

Nell begins to defend herself and he counters with a lecture about being a responsible employee and how she isn't even wearing a uniform, and rather than continue to listen, she opens the screen, throws the pizza at the man, then storms down the walkway to her car. Which is being ticketed by a cop. She half-heartedly attempts to flirt her way out of the fine, but the officer isn't going for it, and so she snatches the ticket from him with a defeated sigh, opens the passenger door, and climbs back into the driver's seat. She opens the glove compartment and shoves the ticket in with what appears to be a dozen others. Then she tries to start the engine, which won't turn over. She tries a couple more times, screaming and swearing and banging her head on the steering wheel, until her tantrum is interrupted by a hard knock on the window. She looks up, startled. It's the dude with the pizza, and he's psychotically angry.

Next scene

Nell, now carrying the heels she'd been tiptoeing around in, is walking down the street of a much dirtier neighborhood. Men catcall and playfully reach for her as she walks by, and she glares at them. She's got a sad, wet pizza box tucked under one arm with an empty plastic gasoline container perched on top. Her tights are ripped, and her hair has dried awkwardly. She lets herself into a tiny apartment, kicking clothes and garbage out of the way as she tries to get in the door. The apartment is messy in a calculated kind of way: paintings and artwork lean against the walls, hundreds of books are stacked on the floor and on chairs, and piles of clothes and takeout containers are scattered across the floor. There's what appears to be an unmade futon in one corner of the room, and in the corner opposite there is a desk that has a nice computer and a bunch of electronic equipment balanced on it.

She sets the pizza box on the floor and plops down on what looks like a large pile of blankets on top of the futon, but that pile screams in pain before shoving her roughly to the floor. We see that there had been a gentleman sleeping under those blankets, and Nell turns around, incredulous. "You broke up with me"—*dramatic pause*—"WHILE SLEEPING IN MY FUCK-ING BED?!" she screams, and we see a look pass between them. It registers on both faces that she is going to punch him. She takes a big swing and barely grazes his jaw, as he jumps out of the way just in time to avoid major damage. He clambers out of the bed in his underwear, trying to get his clothes on as Nell desperately chases him on her knees trying to land a punch. He dances out of the way of her fists, and she's still on the floor chasing him on her knees, while Foot Locker apologizes and tries to explain. She resorts to throwing random trash at his head, finally making contact when she lobs the empty plastic gas can. "Why do you even have that?" he asks, rubbing the spot on his head where it hit him. He's still without pants and in his Foot Locker jersey.

"My car broke down, and I was going to get some gas to put in it to see if that fixed it. But I'm tired. And it was raining. So I just left it in the middle of the street."

They have a discussion about how she hadn't come home the night before, hence delivering pizzas in a party dress, and how he's done having fun and wants to settle down. With someone else. He puts his pants on and wishes her well, saying, "Don't stalk me," as he puts on his coat. Right before he goes he hands her an envelope and says, "This was posted on your door earlier." Foot Locker leaves, and Nell turns the envelope over in her lap to reveal to the camera an eviction notice. She pulls a wad of folded bills from her bra, mostly ones, and counts them. Then she reaches for the pizza box.

Next scene

It's morning, and Nell is sitting at her desk in pajamas, coffee cup in hand. She's wearing a headset with a microphone that is covered in duct tape and is frantically fiddling with wires and clicking the computer mouse. She introduces her radio personality, explains how listeners can either call in or e-mail their questions for her to answer, and also gives them a PayPal address to which they can send donations. There's a sticky note taped to her computer monitor that says: "Total donations so far: $37.52." On the desk is a legal pad with a long list of bills and expenses, a small pile of crumpled money on top of it. We hear her first caller begin to cry and explain her dilemma and then suddenly the equipment goes out. Nell scrambles and frantically unplugs a bunch of cords and wires while muttering curses and griping about how she needs an IT person to help with her show, and by the time she gets everything up and running again her time is up and she has to apologize and beg the audience to tune in next week.

Next scene

Later that day, dressed in the same pajamas, Nell is sitting in a coffee shop with a laptop and a pile of mail. Her friend Calvin glides in, impeccably dressed, and joins her at the table after charming the barista and several female customers.

"Is this a housewarming?" he asks, motioning to all the stuff she has piled on the table. "Sort of," Nell replies, then shows him the eviction notice. Calvin is a banker, and he starts in on Nell with a complicated lecture about mutual funds and retirement plans and how she's too old to be living her life this way. After going through bills and bank statements they figure out that she is $15,000 in debt and has $90 cash, $50 in the bank, plus the $37.52 in donations.

Nell asks if she can live in Calvin's guest room, and he scoffs and says absolutely not, (1) because she's a slob, and (2) because she would get in the way of his dating action. Crestfallen, she tearfully explains that she doesn't have anywhere to go, and Calvin has a pitying look on his face that makes it seem like he's changing his mind about letting her move in. "I'm going to help you," he says earnestly, and she looks up hopefully as he gets up to jog across the coffee shop and grab one of the free weekly papers on the other side of the room. He sets it down in front of her and opens to a page of "rooms for rent" listings. "I'll pay for the first month," he offers, peeling hundreds off a roll of them that he pulls from inside his blazer. "And use the rest to hire some college kids to move all your shit. I threw my fucking back out last time. FOUR MONTHS AGO." Calvin excuses himself to go hit on the barista in earnest, and Nell pulls out a marker and starts circling ads and dialing numbers on her cell phone. The first number is a sex chat line, and at first she recoils in horror but then after a couple of seconds starts simulating sex with the person on the other end of the phone, loudly. So loudly that Calvin comes over to snatch the phone away and starts making the calls himself. After mumbling into the phone for what seems like a split second he hangs up and announces, "I found you a place to live. Finish your latte."

Next scene

Calvin's sleek black luxury vehicle cruises down a very familiar-looking street. From inside the car we see Nell staring out the passenger window with a confused look on her face. "There are no crack houses in this neighborhood, who the fuck over here needs to rent out a goddamned room?"

Calvin responds, "Some old guy needed to give up his man cave and is renting it out for fifty bucks a week" and slows down as they pass Nell's car, now covered in tickets and wearing a bright yellow boot, then stops completely just beyond it. "Go see the room," he admonishes, "I'll wait here." Nell checks the address Calvin had written on a napkin ("Don't lose that; I wrote that girl's number on it!") and groans as she gets out of the car, the light of recognition dawning in her eyes. She trudges up the walk and hesitates before raising her hand to knock, tapping her foot nervously. After a few awkward seconds of her turning to make faces at Calvin, who is ignoring her and texting on his phone in the car, the door opens. There stands pizza dude. And he looks pissed.

The end

good (food) in bed

· ·

having diarrhea all the time is the worst

MASHED POTATOES THAT HOPEFULLY WON'T HURT YOUR BUTTHOLE

Gather

    1 bag of yellow potatoes

    1 can of low-sodium broth

    a little butter substitute, like Earth Balance, if your
       tummy can handle it

    salt and pepper

    dried basil

1. Quarter the potatoes and cover them in a big pot with cold water. Bring it to a low boil and keep it going until they're fork-tender. Drain.

2. Return the potato chunks to the hot pot and use a masher to smash them to whatever consistency suits you. I like mine a little lumpy, but I'm technically a garbage can, so you do what you want. Just know that unless you spend a lot of time in the gym on arm day, it's never gonna be perfectly smooth and you know what? It's fine.

3. As you stir with one hand, slowly trickle in broth with the other. There's no amount that's too much or too little; I err on the side of less liquid because I don't want it to turn to soup, but I don't want to choke on coarse potato chunks, either. If you want, you can add some Earth Balance at this point, too, to make it kind of creamy and buttery. Once you've grown exhausted from constant stirring, season with salt and pepper and some basil.

EASILY DIGESTIBLE BANANA PANCAKES

You need

1 medium ripe (but not brown) banana (as a diarrhea person, I always have bananas)

⅛ teaspoon baking powder

¼ teaspoon vanilla extract

2 eggs

1. Peel the banana and break it up in a bowl. Use a fork to thoroughly grind it up and continue mashing until

the banana has the consistency of yogurt and you've worked out all the big lumps. This should yield ⅓ to ½ cup of mashed bananas. Add the baking powder (for fluffiness) and vanilla (for vanillaness).

2. Whisk the eggs together, then pour them over the banana and stir until the eggs are completely combined. The batter is gonna be pretty loose, like your bowels.

3. Heat a few spritzes of cooking spray in a frying pan. Drop a couple of heaping tablespoons of batter onto the hot griddle. I hate making pancakes, because they're a huge mess and I never know when to flip the shits over without glopping it all over the stove, but with these I just lift a corner after a couple of minutes to make sure the underside is brown and then wiggle one of those skinny, springy spatulas under them kinda slowly and then gently slide it off. Cook for another minute. I'm a rapid-fire grilled cheese flipper, and I typically implement that same strategy here: once I've got a good golden color on each side I flip constantly because the threshold between perfect and burnt beyond recognition is unpredictable and I don't wanna miss my window. So flip these a lot until they look good.

4. If I'm in the middle of a Crohn's flare-up, I don't use anything on top of these, but I'm sure they are a delicious vehicle for butter and syrup or whipped cream or peanut butter. Or fruit, I guess, if you're one of those health people.

RICE PUDDING FOR SAD BUTTS

Ingredients

3 cups almond milk

1 cup white rice, uncooked (I know brown is better for you but that fiber is PAINFUL)

¼ cup sugar

1 teaspoon vanilla extract

¼ teaspoon almond extract

cinnamon, to taste

1. This is criminally easy and you can make it even when you're weak and dehydrated from shooting your brains out your asshole. Combine the almond milk and the rice in a 2- to 3-quart saucepan, and bring it to a boil.

2. Reduce heat and simmer for half an hour with a lid on it—or a large plate if you're like me and bought pots without lids because they were cheaper or accidentally dropped several lids on the concrete steps during your last move—until the rice is soft. Stir in the sugar, both extracts, and a pinch of cinnamon.

EASY CHICKEN SOUP THAT
DOESN'T HAVE THAT GROSS CAN SKIN

Okay, so this is one of those things you make when you've stopped pooping liquid fire but aren't yet ready to dive face-first into a pizza. Like, celery isn't really on my list of "things that process through my system without feeling like I've swallowed a box of rusty nails," so I gotta wait for a few white bread days to pass without incident before I attempt to test-drive a carrot, but once I pass that first solid turd, it's on.

Procure

    1 tablespoon butter
    ½ cup chopped onion
    ½ cup chopped celery
    1 box chicken broth
    1 can vegetable broth
    ½ pound cooked chicken, chopped or picked apart,
        whatever works
    1½ cups egg noodles
    1 cup sliced carrots
    ½ teaspoon dried basil
    ½ teaspoon dried oregano
    salt and pepper, to taste

LOOK HOW SIMPLE THIS IS. In a large pot over medium heat, melt butter. Cook onion and celery in butter for five minutes. Pour in the broths and stir in chicken, noodles, carrots, basil, oregano, salt, and pepper. Bring to a boil, then reduce heat and simmer twenty minutes.

Pharmacy shopping list

    Imodium
    Pepto-Bismol
    saltines
    diet Gatorade
    Tums (tropical flavor, for real)
    Pepcid
    Pedialyte freezer pops

apple juice

broth

pretzels

Beano

a copy of *The New Yorker* and *Vanity Fair*, because you'll
actually have time to read them—on the toilet.

milk and oreos

I fucking love white people. As a matter of fact, having grown up surrounded by their legion on the rough, tree-lined streets of Chicago's North Shore, I wasn't really even aware that I wasn't white until I was approximately seven years old. Okay, I knew, because I never had a sunburn, whatever the fuck that is, but I didn't know-know. But with every politely declined camping invitation and spat-out mouthful of roasted beets, it became that much clearer to me that, despite my penchant for craft beers and J.Jill knit cardigans, I AM NOT WHITE.

It has been exceptionally difficult for me to come to terms with this shocking revelation. I don't know what the fuck Kwanzaa is. If a bitch asks me some black history shit, I'm always like, "I don't fucking know! Rosa Parks?" And black people are always telling me I "talk white," which until recently I thought was due to my passionate defense of Christopher Guest films but now realize is a criticism of the fact that when I say "mother-fucker," I pronounce the *th*. And the *-er*.

I'm pretty much an expert in white people. I don't really understand lacrosse, but I do pay for a subscription to *The New Yorker*. The subtle differences between us, though, were the catalyst through which I became cognizant of my blackness: The stay-at-home mom who also has a nanny? The shorts in the middle of December?! I don't get it, but I'm grateful for you guys, I really am. Without white people I wouldn't know what the fuck a scone is. Or that a $5,000 bicycle is a real thing. And with Valentine's Day fast approaching, I thought I would write them a love letter to prove my undying affection for their kind.

Dear white people,

I love you because you fucking mean well. I should clarify and say that I am referring to white people who buy North Face jackets and take their babies to yoga class, NOT these fucking Newport-smoking teen moms named Destiny, spelled with nine e's. Those kinds of white people are terrifying. I like farmers' market white people, the ones who are always dressed like they just finished climbing K2 when all they've done all day is eat samples at Whole Foods. The ones who try to convince me that a $15 jar of organically grown, locally sourced, environmentally sustainable white peach marmalade is a worthwhile fucking purchase. I'm black, ho. FUCK EARTH. Black people don't really believe in recycling. Or, for that matter, artisanal jam. If you see me put my Coke can in the recycling bin, it's because (1) someone left that shit within arm's reach of my desk and (2) a white person is watching me. Seriously, if there weren't so many white people around all the time I would literally be standing outside with a can of hair spray spraying that shit at the goddamned sun. Fuck being cold. The only black vegans I can think of are the ones dodging the bags of donated oatmeal raining down on them from Red Cross helicopters, but I love that about you guys, I love that you could sit down to an enormous Thanksgiving dinner and only eat the fucking green beans because a turkey with a brain the size of my toenail didn't have a happy childhood. That shit is fucking admirable.

I also love you because you are still afraid of black people. Whether or not you are the type of misguided racial profiler who would lock the doors as I walk uncomfortably close to that old-ass piece-of-shit Volvo you're sitting in, if I raised my voice in here right now two-thirds of you would get out your wallets and start up a collection to get me my reparations. Or whatever it is colored people are always YELLING ABOUT.

I love that you're so fucking fancy. You don't cram yourselves into a sticky booth at IHOP to shovel four-dollar pancakes from a box mix down your throats, no, you stand huddled against the cold for three hours waiting for the hotly anticipated opening of that adorable new brunch place that serves bald eagle omelets and tiger milk pancakes with cinnamon butter. And I'm snarling at the table next to yours, sneering as you upload a snapshot of your breakfast and tap-tap-tap out a glowing Yelp review, but that's just bitter jealousy because your three-year-old is trading mutual funds on his iPad at the table and I only have thirty-seven dollars in my 401(k).

I love you because you love me. If white guilt were tangible currency I'd be in the 1 percent. I'm sure it's because in your minds I fill the role of the minimally threatening sidekick or the sassy black maid white people have been conditioned by cartoons and television sitcoms to yearn for your entire lives. I am that child-

hood dream actualized: the Tootie to your Blair, the Alfonso to your Ricky, the broom-wielding thick brown ankles to your mischievous mouse-chasing house cat. You love that I can teach you things about black culture and our current sociopolitical landscape, and I love that you have no idea that I don't know what the fuck I'm talking about. I'm not Cornel West, bitch, I don't know shit about black people! I'm from the fucking suburbs! But I have an innate sense of rhythm, so I'm a total blast to take to the disco, yet you can also relax with the knowledge that I'm not going to embarrass you at your wine-and-cheese party by saying "pitcher" when I'm referring to a photograph.

I'm never going to go kayaking, I don't understand the popularity of the show Arrested Development, *and I'm still not sure what Montessori means, but I love you. Let's be together forever and ever. Or at least until a white person becomes president again and you can stop pretending to like me.*

Dear black people,
I love you, too. Sometimes I sound like a Valley girl. A Valley girl with a sinus infection who has taken a cheese grater to her vocal cords, but a Valley girl nonetheless. Rachel says that she loves my voice and its "California diction," although I'm not sure whether that is a compliment considering that I was born in a hospital in suburban Chicagoland. And I love that most of you don't make me feel weird about my voice, even if it differs from yours. Because for some black people it's not enough to just be black. You can't just have brown skin and kinky hair and a wide nose and big lips and a large ass; you have to talk a certain way and think a certain way and present yourself a certain way.

I love you because, in case you didn't know, every third black person you meet is an unofficial scorekeeper in life's never-ending game: "Are you black enough to be black?" If you are black and can't remember ever having received the barometer of real blackness with which you are to measure the downness of your contemporaries, chances are you are the kind of black person who enunciates all of her t's and g's and probably has a Metallica album or two in regular rotation on her iPod. My whole early life was spent seeking out the "other kind" of black people, black people who unabashedly listened to rock music and quoted Star Trek: The Next Generation in regular conversation. Black people who were often accused of "acting white," although no one could ever really explain what that meant. As a kid I never wore blond wigs or bleached my skin, yet every day some wielder of the black-o-meter offered his or her unsolicited assessment that the way I played kickball or foursquare or jumped rope was most decidedly the white way of doing things.

I love you because black people who are uncomfortable in their own skin and with their own identities often try to control and demean other black people by challenging their "blackness." It's an age-old trick. Maybe you won't notice that I'm wrong and an idiot if I deflect and put you on the defensive about your heritage. Because there is no right answer to the question of who's blacker than whom; it's an ideological pissing contest. And a fight, by the way, that the Negro-lite can never win. I love that as I've gotten older there seem to be fewer and fewer of these people in my life, that all the tan and chocolate and coffee complexions in my world seem to all be working together rather than pulling each other apart. I dated a dude who called me a "house nigger" once because I think Tupac is kind of overrated. Oh, for real. A rational person would understand that maybe I just prefer Biggie.

I love you because I grew up in the fucking suburbs, man, with lots of other black kids just like me. That's the reason I speak this way; that's the reason Faith No More is my favorite band; that's the reason I know so many goddamned people named Emily. For me, this is keeping it motherfucking real. I shaved my head because relaxing my hair was destroying my scalp, I got tattooed because they look cool and no one was around to tell me not to. Apparently each racial judge comes equipped with his own specific ruler by which we Uncle Toms get measured. For some, appropriate slang usage is the gauge; for others, style of hair and dress dictate the guidelines. But the kids are figuring it out. I was on the South Side a few weeks ago and saw a black kid on a skateboard wearing purple skinny jeans with his hair locked.

I'm never going to eat hot sauce, I hate going to all-day black gospel church service, and I will never understand the appeal of two pounds of yaki affixed to an otherwise beautiful head of curly black hair, but I love you. Let's be together forever and ever. Now let's go fuck some shit up while we still have this halfrican president who will hopefully pardon our black asses if we ever get caught.

black beauty

I was still a kid when I first figured out that I am ugly. This was in the 1980s, back when there were still real-looking people on prime-time television and magazines weren't saturated with women made of cocaine and Photoshop who set an impossible standard of unobtainable beauty, so it wasn't glaringly obvious what a hideous little beast I was. I can't imagine being a female child in this new millennium in which half-naked celebrity ass is perfectly acceptable and readily available on the sides of buses and shit. I am a slave to sugar and cheese and totally in love with this new trend of putting bacon on every goddamned thing on the menu, and I have never been shy around a plate of food, but if I was seventeen years old and basically a walking open wound and I was being bombarded by images that reinforce the idea that, as I am, I'm not good enough, I'd have a fucking eating disorder. Bulimia probably, because anorexia requires the kind of restraint and self-control that, as evident by the thunderous clap of these thighs, I am obviously lacking.

We were pretty poor, and most of our food came from boxes and cans. I should specify, before your minds start to fill with television images of the barred windows and chain-link fences meant to contain overpopulated housing project developments teeming with children whose only option is potato chips for breakfast, that I grew up in a really nice suburb. We had art in school. And music. A swimming pool. Fucking tennis courts. My mother had a college education, but she was severely disabled, and the two of us lived on less than eight hundred dollars a month in government aid. When survival is your imperative, what you look like while doing so becomes of increasingly diminishing importance.

"Samantha is ugly and smells like pee" was the reason some kid gave for not wanting to be spelling partners with me one afternoon. Now, I'm not so arrogant that I won't entertain an opinion contrary to my own, and, considering my Salvation Army clothing and overall disheveled appearance, I conceded that the kid might have a goddamned point. I was ugly. I could never find pants that fit me at Kids "R" Us. And I probably *did* smell like pee. It was true, and it didn't bother me all that much. I mean, it sort of did, because we are reminded from birth that girls are supposed to be pretty and delicate, but I came to terms with my ugliness relatively quickly. I knew that if I was ever to be rescued from a goddamned tower, Prince Charming better have done some motherfucking push-ups beforehand.

Being ugly affords you a unique sort of freedom, and as I progressed through school I became more comfortable with how effortless some aspects of life are when you aren't considered physically attractive. Eating whatever you want is fucking amazing. So is being able to shave your head at sixteen because you're goddamned sick of curling irons. You can be a jerky smart-ass without having to worry about offending someone who might otherwise want to stick his dick in you. I went to school with a lot of gorgeous girls, girls who breathlessly recounted their first kisses and first blow jobs and first sexual experiences to me between classes. It stung, for sure, because the potential sexual interest of postpubescent young men is the currency of female youth, and to never have been kissed as a junior in high school was fucking devastating. But beauty is this fixed thing. At least conventionally, and either your face and body are constructed in a way that fits those parameters or they aren't. It's pretty clear whether you are or are not beautiful, and the availability of your Friday nights are an indicator that will clear up any confusion. When you decidedly ARE NOT there isn't much you can do to change it, unless magic is a real thing. And don't get me wrong, I wasn't some soulless cyborg who was immune to the fact that I spent entire weekends in my room listening to Tori Amos and reading. But once I'd drawn the conclusion that the face and body I was born with were the reason why I had so much extra study time, I tried to stop feeling so bad about it. Because really, what can you do?

I was diagnosed with Crohn's disease when I was twenty-five, which, as autoimmune diseases go, is one of the least glamorous of the bunch. It has ruined my joints and causes me to have diarrhea all the fucking time, and I'm not sure if there is anything less beautiful than a woman with a jammed-up colon limping along ten feet behind you while shitting an adult diaper. I'm not such an asshole that I don't at least attempt to tuck it in and wrap it up and slap a pretty bow on it. Even as hopeless as my physical situation might sometimes be, right now I have a little BB cream on to even out my complexion and a Spanx stretched from my ass to right up under my goddamned bra. Because it seems too sad to just not give a *total* shit.

I'm not sure that there is a time that I really feel beautiful. I still have the same face, the same lazy eye that is a dead give-away when I'm tired, the same skin beard, the same weird dark spots and unexpected patches of hair. At thirty-two I still haven't matured enough to not enjoy the validation of someone wanting to get naked in my bed. If I somehow can club a decent-looking dude over the head and drag him back to my apartment, I still don't feel particularly beautiful. Proud of myself? Yes. Irritated that I still kind of feel like shit and that this dude who could've given me chlamydia hasn't solved a single one of my problems? Absolutely. But I do always feel smart and funny and brave.

A couple of weeks ago Jill and I went to a dating class. It was held at the Discovery Center, a learning annex home to educational courses such as, but not limited to: Classic French Cooking, Past-Life Regression, Bartending Certification, and Sensual Chair Dance. A class was listed in its fall catalog that seemed too goddamned amazing to pass up: Black Women's Dating Boot Camp, a dating guide "for women who want to find their groove." From the description offered on the website: "As the roles of men and women evolve, it becomes harder and harder for black men and black women to define their needs, desires and to find a committed, caring relationship with each other. In this seminar you will learn how to successfully determine your personal relationship style, and that of the perfect man for you. In addition you will discover a method to beat the odds against black women finding dates, mates, and marriage. This class is for Afro-American women who want to find their one great date, mate, or marriage partner." Despite the use of the outdated term Afro-American (where are we again? 1978?!) my vagina swelled with romantic possibility.

It was promised that we would "discover the three essential ingredients for a perfect relationship," "learn how slavery, race, and religion impact dating," and "learn why the smart ones 'love the one they're with,'" among other important things. And all within two and a half miraculous hours. And all for the low, low price of forty dollars, plus material fees. So I could be an asshole and say that I signed up solely for the joke of the whole thing. Because, let's face it, expecting to figure out why I haven't yet found my groove after two and a half hours with a strange woman to whom I am totally going to lie when faced with any uncomfortable questions that might lend some insight into why I'm perpetually single is kind of a joke. But there is a part of me, a big part, a significant part, that was really hoping to gain (dare I say it?) some insight.

Because my bitch-ass friends lie to me. Yes, they do. And don't feel bad for me, because your bitch-ass friends lie to you, too. It isn't intentional or necessarily malicious; it's just fucking reflexive. They totally mean well. Example:

Sam: I am too fucking fat for this tight, shiny shirt, ugh. *(Struggles to remove self from said tiny blouse while stumbling out of dressing room and away from the glare of its unflattering full-length mirrors.)*

Sam's bitch-ass lying whorefriend, *without looking up from her iPod and/or cell phone and/or Kindle*: No, you are not,

girl. You are the most beautiful person I know. Goddamn,
Sudoku is hard!

Sam, *fat arms stuck above head tangled in sleeves of shiny shirt,
which is now caught on bra hook and won't budge from around
shoulder and keeps making little ripping noises with every attempt
to blindly dislodge self from shirt she* already knew *was not the
move, and paying for a too-small shirt because it ripped in half
is fucking humiliating*: These doll clothes are not made for
a normal body. Fuck it, I'm on a diet starting right now.

Friend, *flipping through magazine and/or updating Facebook
status and/or intently reapplying eyeliner and not paying attention to Sam at all*: Stop that, you're beautiful. You're perfect.
And that shirt looks amazing.

Sam, *sliding back and forth on floor trying to use the carpet trac-
tion to shimmy shirt over head without (1) shredding an expensive
blouse, or (2) starting a class A combustible fire*: JUST SAY I'M
TOO BIG FOR IT, YOU IDIOT, AND PULL THIS
FUCKING SHIRT OFF ME.

Every time I'm mourning the death of what I once believed
had been a serendipitous romance, or pouting, disconsolate,
because some clandestine relationship will never come to frui-
tion, my go-to method of self-flagellation is "He doesn't love
you because you are not pretty." Oh, brother. "If you fixed your
teeth he'd stop seeing other people." Yes, obviously. And then
I get in bed with a pile of magazines and shame myself for not
having the willpower to subsist on steamed broccoli and lemon

water alone. Thumbing through pages of cute shit from sizes small to extra-extra small, I wonder why I haven't yet invested in an assistant whose job it is to follow me around with professional lighting. And an IV fluid bag because, seriously, I could stand to do a better job of properly hydrating.

The dating class was held at 7:00 p.m. on a Friday, perfect for lonely, downtrodden women who wouldn't be otherwise occupied or out on a date with an actual human male. I had my friend Kathleen's car and drove into the city after work, getting there twenty-five minutes early, which is a lifetime in a tiny fucking Honda. Instead of going in and making myself comfortable in the seat farthest back and closest to the door, I decided to sit across the street, steaming up the car and texting in the dark like a creep. I figured I could watch my new sisterfriends as they approached the building. Size them up, assessing whether their outfits were cuter than the one that had taken me two whole minutes to put together.

Here is what I was expecting: a warm and wise black woman, firm but fair like Oprah, possibly wearing a headwrap and large ethnic jewelry. No, *definitely* wearing a headwrap, with a dreadlock or two poking out. And giant turquoise rings. Maybe something with an African print? And she was totally going to smell like sandalwood oil and incense. This was a woman who carried her babies close to her breast in a cloth sling, people. A WOMAN WHO MADE HER OWN YOGURT. I anticipated making a dozen new best friends! Empowered black women who, oops, I mean *Afro-American* women, who had bonded over our mutual dissatisfaction with the state of modern romance, and commiserated over the surprising lack of beauty products for black women with natural hair to be found in major retail stores.

The day before my senior year of high school started I asked my sister Carol to shave off all my hair. Up to that point the trajectory of my hair journey mirrored that of most black girls: baby hair in little poufs or braids, hot combs and curling irons when I learned how not to squirm in the stylist's chair, chemical relaxers as soon as I was of age. I was not offered a choice in the matter. Besides, it was the 1980s and that is just what you *did* back then. And I was not born to the kind of woman who wore cowrie shells and Bantu knots. Grace Irby straightened her hair and dyed it a brazen red not found in nature. She smoked cigarettes, used Olay, shaved off her eyebrows only to pencil in new ones that were a closer match to her bottled hair color, and wore red lipstick every minute she was awake. A child of the forties, this was most certainly not a woman who was going to allow her young daughter to walk around sporting coarse virgin hair. When we didn't have money for the beauty shop, which was often, I spent my Sunday evenings slumped over in a hard-backed kitchen chair pinning my ears forward while my mom heated those skinny metal combs over the burner of the stove.

I can still hear that sizzle. And I still remember the entire routine: hair washed with Sulfur8, conditioned with Creme of Nature (remember that shit?!) with the plastic cap and hair dryer, rinsed in the sink, blown dry over the course of an hour because that raggedy handheld dryer with the comb attachment kept blowing a goddamned fuse. I would watch TV while parting my hair to oil my scalp with TCB, grease up my ears and hairline to protect against burns, suffer through the indignity of the hot comb, then carefully roll it all up, cover it with a satin cap, and try to get an hour or two of sleep while half sitting up because lying on those curlers was fucking painful, then doze off during class the next day because my pretty hair kept me up all goddamned night.

In middle school I got a relaxer and spent a lot of time both tucking my long, straight hair behind my ears like the white girls I was attempting to emulate and inconspicuously peeling scabs from the chemical burns I'd received as a party favor from my scalp. I haven't had a perm in almost seventeen years, yet I can still smell it in my brain. The fire that blooms inside your nostrils as the first prickle of painful heat kicks up at the nape of your neck. The first one I ever got was done at home, and I sat gripping the relaxer box as my head exploded in pain, eyes blinking away tears and fixated on the soft, bone-straight hair of the woman on the Dark and Lovely box. I was ashamed that my sister had to buy the super strength, for the coarsest hair. But I had been promised long, fine hair that would actually blow in the wind, and all I had to do to get it was sit real still and not touch my head for twenty minutes, even though it felt like it was being burned with a blowtorch. Because my hair wouldn't be beautiful until it looked like it was really *my* hair.

The only real experience I'd had with a black woman wearing her hair naturally was with my seventh-grade guidance counselor. And even though she bucked convention with her tiny Afro and loud outfits, which appealed to my ingrained rebellious streak, I wasn't convinced that it was a look I could pull off. And I didn't want to, because everyone always said shit like "Where's she from, Africa?" As if being from Africa was the worst possible thing. And to kids whose biggest crises arose from not having the right Eddie Bauer book bag, it totally was. But something in me shifted before that last year of school. My hair never looked right, and I couldn't afford to maintain it anyway, so I just shaved it all off. Lucky that I have a decently shaped head. But that was in 1996, when there still weren't a shitload of black girls walking around without hair. And the Internet was this nascent little thing, not the wealth of information full of tips on how to use apple cider vinegar and articles on co-washing it is today.

I wasn't scorned. I wasn't drawn and quartered in the center of town. But I was also sixteen, and people dismissed it as teenage angst manifested. *A phase*, and all that. I'm lazy, and long hair is for people with patience and energy. If I leave it alone for a few months these beautiful, tightly coiled springs sprout from my skull and everyone loves them but even that gets to be too much. So, by default, I'm a part of this movement whether I want to be or not. In my dream life there is this community of women who understand what it means to be a 4C and own diffusers, and we get together and talk about the virtues of coconut oil or whatever. And I'd hoped to meet some of these women in this stupid class.

Here is what I got: Well, what happens to a dream deferred? I sat outside the Discovery Center watching groups of tiny Lincoln Park trixies in fitted black pants skitter down the sidewalk, huddled together against the cold on their way to one of the neighboring bars. No brightly colored head scarves; no neatly plaited Senegalese twists; no luminous brown skin. Jill, who is white and who agreed to take the class for anthropological purposes (and because I strong-armed her into it), arrived and we entered the building to find that we were the only two people who'd signed up for the class. The only two people in a motherfucking dating boot camp for black women, one of whom is

Caucasian, and the other who might as well be. I HAVE A LOT OF DAVE MATTHEWS ON MY IPOD. ★welp★

The syllabus was hardly what I'd been expecting. Instead of spending two hours focusing on rebuilding black families and improving interpersonal relationship between black men and women or whatever fruity hippie pipe dreams I'd been so gassed up about, Jill and I basically sat through a lecture that should have been titled: "How to Catch and Trap a White Man. PS, Don't Have Sex with Any Man Before You Get Ninety Days' Worth of Expensive Dinners and Free Cocktails out of Him. (And Maybe a Concert or a Play.)" Our instructor was nice enough, but flipping through the packet of information she gave us filled me with dread. I wasn't going to learn anything about myself and why my relationships fail so miserably, but she did intend to teach me how to deny my natural loudness and progressive thoughts in favor of adopting the role of a complacent mute in order to impress, not threaten, my ideal mate.

But we're talking about beauty, not my need to assert myself and why I should try to repress that urge around successful men whom I might hope to ensnare in my demure ladytrap. Buried deep into the photocopied pages (this is what my ten dollars paid for?) was a sheet that she somehow skipped during our two-and-a-half-hour intensive session: BEAUTY TIPS. Oh, of course.

THE HIGHLIGHTS

1. Dress sexy, not sleazy.

What does this mean, like, in practice? No lingerie outdoors? No Lucite heels at the dinner table?! I feel like this is a thing we hear all the time, but it doesn't have any real meaning. Okay, I *kind of* know what she's saying. "Don't wear a dress that shows your pussyhole." But come on. One man's ceiling is another man's floor. It's hella confusing! I choose to avoid this conundrum altogether mostly by dressing like a teenage boy.

2. Show off two out of four body parts, but not all four.

WTF, bitch? To what four body parts are you referring? Because unless you are listing each leg and each breast individually, do you really expect a woman not to show her left arm on a date?!

3. Dress youthfully, but not too young.

Again, where is the line and who gets to draw it? Also, I'm pretty sure this forty-plus-year-old woman might have been wearing those low-slung sweatpants with words across the butt. Ninety percent sure.

4. Don't wear rings.

Get a NuvaRing instead, maybe?

5. Be clean and well made up.

Do you really have to tell women who had fifty bucks to blow on a frivolous dating class to take a goddamned shower? PS, I've had sex with a number of dudes who didn't notice the green shit I scraped out of my belly button under my fingernails, or the dirt on the bottom of my sandal feet. They really couldn't care less.

6. Dress in a manner that fits in with your cub's crowd.

Just, ew. My cub? Seriously?! I NEED A MOTHERFUCKING

BEAR. And if it matters to a man that your style of clothing fits in with his crowd, he is moist. And he hangs out with dicks.

7. Skirts are more flattering than pants.

I better perfect the art of smiling and nodding, too. Also, I should probably be somewhere washing dishes or something.

8. Men love long, shiny hair. Try to keep your hair long.

Shit. I'm fucked.

9. Color your gray hair. Gray hair is aging.

Double fucked.

10. Make sure your teeth are as white and straight as possible.

Triple fucking fucked! I swear to God, though, if I hit the lottery or sell more than thirty copies of this goddamned book I will *seriously consider* adult braces. But then I also have to quit my job, because I can't spend my entire day explaining to people why a bitch who's old enough to take Prevacid every day is suddenly wearing headgear.

11. Ditch the eyeglasses.

BUT I NEED THEM TO SEE, OMG.

12. Men fall in love with their eyes!!! Be eye candy!

I am obviously going to die alone. With short gray hair. In a sleazy outfit that exposes my slutty right kneecap.

the many varieties of hospital broth

I haven't been in the hospital with a flare-up in over a year. Which is a major feat considering that at one point in my history I was there so often the nurses knew my name and what I was there for without having to look it up and shit. I'd just walk into the ER with my overnight bag and they'd be all, "Let me warm up the CT scanner. Grrrrrl. You still prefer vegetable broth? Let me get your room ready." I haven't written about the charred wasteland that is my intestines enough lately, and I'm sure that's keeping most of you who know me up at night with worry. So let's talk some shit.

2013 marks the eighth year of living with this dreaded Crohn's disease, and for the first time in a long time I've been feeling pretty good on a regular basis. Two summers ago I was totally stressed the fuck OUT: working all the time, not taking good enough care of myself, keeping people in my life who drove me fucking apeshit, and that stress manifested itself into one big giant knot dead in the center of my stomach, followed by a week spent flat on my back watching *Up* and *The Time Traveler's Wife* on constant repeat while getting shot up with Dilaudid and steroids and insulin. Because although a bitch is not diabetic, too much Prednisone sent your girl into diabetic shock. HOLY SHIT.

It's nearly impossible to sleep when you're in the goddamned hospital. I go to a really nice one where I get my own room and my own cable television and my very own personal assistant to help change my shitty diapers and flip my pillow over or whatever else I am too lazy, or entangled in tubes, to do for myself. Anyway, it's 2:00 a.m. and I'm on so many drugs and have a port in my arm and I had dozed off sitting up like your granny does, and four nurses come crashing into my room and shake me awake because apparently I've stopped breathing and a bunch of alarms are ringing and bitches are shouting, and they're yanking my gowns off, and all I could think was "How smelly is my underwear right now?!" while they're shooting shit into my veins and holding the oxygen mask down on my face. I fully expected to go into cardiac arrest, because I don't know if anyone's ever told them, but shaking a bitch awake at 2:00 a.m. in a hospital is some terrifying shit. When all the drama died down I couldn't have cared less about my blood sugar or my inflamed intestines, I was just mad that they'd *cut off* a FIFTY-DOLLAR GODDAMNED BRA. It pisses me off just thinking about it.

One of the problems with not dying in the hospital is that real life still goes on outside those sterilized walls. The cat needed to be fed! My dry cleaning needed to be picked up!! My DIRECTV bill needed to be paid!!! I never end up in the hospital right after the ONE TIME I clean my goddamned apartment every year, and after my sister went to my apartment to rescue Helen Keller and drop her off at the kennel she called my room and was like, "Are you okay? I mean, is your life okay?! How could you be living like this?!" Listen, bitch, had I known I was going to need for anyone other than that cat to see what I do with my empty beer cans, I would have maybe taken out the recycling. Just step over the piles of laundry and magazines and get the fuck out lest you set off any of my booby traps. I know that's how I'm going to die, surrounded by all my poor choices and bad habits. But at least if you're dead, people feel guilty about talking shit about the porn you don't even bother hiding anymore.

I was there for a week. Graduated from ice chips to broth, to broth with three peas in it, to broth with three peas and one noodle in it, to applesauce, to please let me the fuck out of here; this shit is costing me $10,000 a motherfucking day. On release day everyone is extra super nice, skipping into my room with the menu that people with broken legs get to choose from and sneaking me extra apple juices. The "intestinal distress" menu looks something like this: a variety of unsalted broths, apple or cranberry juice, Jell-O that I never order, black coffee, and textureless oatmeal soup. "Who in the hell gets to order chocolate cake and roast beef while they're in the hospital?!" I asked the patient care technician who stood awaiting my food order. "Really?! FRIED CHICKEN DINNER?! Who gets *that* shit?!" She smiled patiently and said, "What about a hard-boiled egg? You can have that. You want a piece of dry white toast with it?" What a tease. No, asshole, I want a double fucking cheeseburger with it, not some goddamned, piece of shit, dry white toast.

But I just snapped the menu shut and said, "For seventy thousand dollars, I want *two* pieces of dry white toast." All of you people who shit normally don't know just how lucky you have it. Next time you feel like complaining about something dumb, I want you to think, "OATMEAL SOUP." See how awesome your life is? That nasty little feeling right there is called perspective.

In October I vomited down the front of my sweater while talking to this woman about prescription dog food, but until then I'd been feeling perfectly fine. Well, diarrhea-every-few-days perfectly fine, but fine nonetheless. That warranted a trip to the ER, where I got two bags of fluids, some Zofran, and some Dilaudid: my feel-better cocktail. I was only there for a few hours, which means that either I was doing pretty well or that my insurance was like GET THAT BITCH OUT OF THERE RIGHT GODDAMNED NOW OR WE AIN'T PAYING *SHIT.*

There's no known cure for Crohn's. I just keep dutifully taking my pills and trying not to drink so much and trying even harder to stay away from fancy French cheeses. Right now I'm not on steroids or rheumatoid arthritis drips, and I'm no longer on immunosuppressive drugs, either. I haven't had to *depend* on special undergarments (see what I did there?!) in months. No rubber sheets. No scopes, no X-rays, no scans, no colonoscopies, NOTHING. And the only thing that has really changed in the last year—because, let's face it, I still get drunk and stress out sometimes—is that I haven't been messing around with any goddamned DUDES. Celibacy cured my shit disease. Alert the *New England Journal of Medicine.*

Seriously, man. It can't be a fucking coincidence! We already know that when I raised my fucking standards a while back it all but dried up my romantical prospects. For reals. And I was a little salty about it at the time, yes, but what an amazing trade-off. Swapping raggedy knuckle–dragging assholes for a clean bill of health for my own precious asshole?! YES, PLEASE. Every time I've saddled myself to some lie-faced, underperforming, whack-piece-of-shit "boyfriend," I've ended up in the hospital two or three or ten times during the course of said relationship. I need to call my hot butt doctor and tell him why my camera endoscopy had unclear results. Because ASSHOLE SONOFABITCH obviously doesn't show up on an intestinal radiograph. This is a revolutionary medical breakthrough I'm making here, people. Think of all the money I could've saved! All those colonoscopies I could've avoided! The first time I had a barium series I wanted to slice my wrists open on the goddamned table. If the doctor would have said, "Listen, bitch, you can avoid being subjected to another one of these if you just get rid of that human garbage texting some other broad out in the waiting room," I would have done so in a HEARTBEAT.

Who knew that not having to worry about the state of my pubic hair at any given moment would result in no longer shitting myself in public? I'd never talk to another person AGAIN if it meant I could stop spending half my paycheck on maintenance drugs. FOR CEREAL. Besides, sex is boring and totally gross. And I'm obviously growing up, despite whatever reflection my ailing credit score might be of my adulthood, because every time I think about banging I just think, GONORRHEA, and about how I don't have it. And about how other people *do*. And about how easily I could catch it. Especially now that there's a drug-resistant strain of that shit. Sex is stressful and ridden with disease and people are soul-sucking opportunists just waiting to rob or betray you, so is it really that surprising that now that I don't have to worry about blemishing my otherwise perfect STD tests that my stomach doesn't hurt all the fucking time?

I'm just saying. Constantly worrying about who a dude is calling when he takes his cell phone into my bathroom in the middle of the night equals SHITSPLOSIVE RAGING STOMACH PAIN DIARRHEA BUTT DISEASE. See also: when he doesn't call me back, or sees me only once a month, or hits on my friends, or fucks wrong, or basically does any of the million things some asshole could do to make me want to hit him with my car. Meanwhile, only having to worry about what time *Real Housewives of Atlanta* is coming on equals I HAVEN'T BEEN SICK FOR A GODDAMNED YEAR. I finally have something to say to these jerks who keep asking why I ain't got no mans. "Well, yes, nosy bitch I went to high school with, I most certainly would like to be married with six and a half children and a golden retriever right now. But, you see, it turns out that I have a physiological reaction to men and their insipid nonsense. Relationships give me baby guts. It's downright dreadful. I'm lucky to even be alive."

So that's that. I'm not horrible and intolerable and physically unappealing. Men don't hate me and think I'm stupid. I'M JUST ALLERGIC TO ASSHOLES. Man, I'm so relieved. And so is my asshole.

the terror of love

I am missing the first bicuspid on the upper right side of my mouth. Eight years ago I got a root canal. It was routine, I guess? How the shit can you know unless you have a skull X-ray machine in your living room? Anyway, I hadn't seen a dentist in fucking forever because dental care is super expensive and while teeth are easily the thing a person is most afraid to fucking lose, ain't nobody got hundreds of dollars just lying around for annual X-rays and cleanings. Besides, I was twenty-five; was I really expected to worry about my goddamned teeth?! I AM YOUNG AND I AM GOING TO LIVE FOREVER BECAUSE HOT POCKETS ARE TOTALLY NUTRITIOUS.

Okay, so I woke up one morning in the gigantic apartment I had stupidly rented at the insistence of my then boyfriend who SWORE TO GOD that he would come over and spend the night more if he didn't have to tiptoe around to avoid pissing off my roommate (he hadn't yet fulfilled this promise, but four months isn't really that long is it? GAH, fuck that guy), and my mouth was hurting. Like, really hurting. Like, I walked past the fan in the kitchen window and almost collapsed in pain when a cool spring breeze hit the raw, exposed nerve also known as my goddamned mouth. I called a dentist from the phone book— because eight years ago there was still such a thing as a fucking phone book—and she called a pharmacist and two hours later I was on the bus clutching a bag filled with antibiotics and Tylenol 3 on my way home to "take it easy" and "try not to eat anything sweet or cold." A couple of days after that? On my back squinting into a blinding fluorescent light while this very nice woman talked to me about her toddler in a soothing voice as she drilled an access hole into my infected tooth and removed all the pulp and rot and mildewing beef gristle.

Last summer I was eating my lunch alone in the darkened conference room at work, crying softly to myself in ecstasy at the deliciousness of the pulled pork wrap I had just purchased from Pret A Manger, when suddenly I felt something hard and jagged on my tongue. Undeterred by what I assumed were the lost fingernails of a careless fast-food worker, I continued to eat that glorious sandwich, gulping down the gritty ends of some teenaged sandwich maker's stray hairs with fervor. But then the tip of my tongue grazed a sharp stalactite of broken tooth protruding from my upper gum. I dropped my sandwich on the floor (I mourn to this very day) and covered my face while run-walking to the bathroom before anyone could see that I had obviously just tried to EAT MY OWN FUCKING FACE. I pulled up my lip to reveal the dentition of a feral street beast: broken shards of mangled tooth and bone littering a tongue that oozed fresh blood and bits of partially chewed slow-roasted pork. My new dentist took an X-ray of my skull and informed me that the dark gray rain cloud I'd thought was a lazy hygienist resting her thumb on the machine was in fact a fist-size clot of bacteria slowly eating its way through my upper jaw.

After googling what "endodontist" meant, I went and saw one and then immediately decided I was too fucking poor to afford $3,000 in root therapy (or whatever the shit is called), and I went back to the regular dentist and let him stand with one foot on my chest and the other braced against the chair while he blackened my right eye trying to break what was left of my busted tooth loose from my skull. That is the worst sound I have ever heard, the crack and separation of bone from *inside my own fucking head*. Tears slid from my eyes involuntarily; I am convinced that this is what hell feels like, the soundtrack of a continuous loop of your head bones breaking in surround sound. I was sent home with a leaky maw packed with gauze stained pink by blood and mouth goo, instructed not to drink anything from a straw for several hours. I iced my face with a tub of pineapple sherbet and texted my friends to bring me soup while gingerly probing my facehole's tender new vacancy with the tip of my tongue.

I'm sitting in Metropolis on Granville at a table in the back near the bathroom so that in case I have sudden-onset diarrhea or drop my three-fourths-full latte in my lap and the MOST DESPERATE THIEF IN THE HISTORY OF EARTH needs to steal the netbook I am borrowing from my boss and the approximately $3,875 worth of lip gloss I have on my person at all times I can, ostensibly, hear him doing so and burst through the door with my pants around my ankles and waddle after him, dripping liquid waste along the way in a fruitless attempt to recover my belongings. I have a date, A REAL DATE, with an actual human. A human who suggested this bustling coffee shop full of college kids and hipster mamas and all I can think about is why I've chosen today of all days to wear my fake tooth. It's something the dentist called a "flipper," a molded piece of plastic that looks like gum tissue with a little bit of tooth poking out.

I get self-conscious about the hole. Hyperaware that when I am laughing really hard and my eyes are crinkled and my belly is shaking that there is this missing piece of my mouth's puzzle. I am glad to be rid of it, for sure, because how lame would it be to drop dead from toxic-blood brain poisoning courtesy of a rotten *tooth* in the twenty-first fucking century? But then I think about meeting this new person, this new person who doesn't know me and might not forgive that six months ago my face was a flesh wound, and I think, LOVE IS TERRIFYING.

The flipper makes me slur my words, badly. And it hurts; the parts that connect it to my upper jaw dig into my gum and it fucking kills. In the mirror it seems totally obvious, almost distracting enough to make me forget the thieves plotting the theft of my $200 virus-riddled computer. The (soy) chai latte I'd ordered was already cold because the flipper didn't rest flush against my jaw and I didn't trust that I could have a normal conversation while dribbling hippie tea from the corner of my mouth. He was scheduled to arrive in three minutes, and I was sweating in the bathroom, using both hands to try to pry this tiny piece of pink-and-white plastic loose from my headbone.

I wear a maxi pad on dates because I am a crazy person and adult human males scare the shit out of me and I'm pretty sure I peed in it a little as a result of the force I was exerting on my poor fucking teeth. They'd already been through so much! I wiped my face with a cold paper towel and pulled my shit together enough to artfully arrange the smart-person books and magazines I just *happened* to be carrying around in my bag. I squinted at my computer screen, at this very essay, wondering how he's going to feel when the book comes out and he realizes that all of this sweaty panic was because of him. We would laugh, obviously, because that's seven months from now and we will already have exchanged house keys and "I love yous" by that point.

He will have already seen the gross, dark line worn into my torso from years of hauling these tits up to my chin with the strength of an underwire; he will already know that I don't really read *The New Yorker* as much as I would like him to believe *today*. By that point my missing tooth will just be a thing we chuckle about as I scrape together my royalties to pay for an implant. So that if this thing doesn't work, and inevitably it won't, I won't have to be terrified ever again. At least not about what my mouth looks like. But he never showed up, so I will never know.

I can't tie a man's necktie. And I love love love that lovely and romantic visual: the adoring wife or girlfriend, face upturned to the glowing sun that is her man's; his body slightly damp and smelling of the shower, of deodorant, of aftershave; white-collared shirt undone at the neck as she playfully tugs at the bolt of brightly colored shiny fabric she had stood in the bedroom doorway watching him struggle with moments before, a smile playing at the corners of her mouth.

Downstairs, there is breakfast made. Maybe not breakfast, because she has to work, too, and who has time for perfectly fried sunny-side-up eggs when there is a management meeting at nine thirty? But the coffee is started and the bialys are defrosting on the counter and the lox from Kaufman's is on the second refrigerator shelf tucked next to the low-fat cream cheese she started buying when his cholesterol numbers came back elevated at his last physical. He showers first, always, because she likes to hit the snooze three or four times, clinging desperately to those precious extra minutes of sleep. She listens to him peeing; she listens to him humming as he lathers shaving cream across the sharp angle of his jaw, carefully and methodically dragging the razor across his cheeks and chin. His slacks and dress shoes have been laid across the overstuffed reclining chair he sometimes likes to watch *The Daily Show* in, after the bottle of wine but before the twenty minutes of reasonably inspired lovemaking. When she hears him fumbling with his toothbrush she takes that as her cue to hustle downstairs and put the coffee on.

This is, like, my fantasy. MY ROMANTIC FANTASY. I don't sit around fucking daydreaming about a dude going down on me for nine hours (BARF) or about riding some massive titanium cock for days at a time (GROSS). What gets *me* hot is all the *other* shit. Dreaming about someone whose allergies I need to remember when I'm at the grocery store: that's where the *real* romance is. Because I've *had* sex before. What a fucking snooze, my dude. Sex is so dumb and boring and unless you're in really incredible shape or you have a ridiculous imagination and are into some really freaky shit, what you do and what I do is limited to a handful of *very* similar things. Even your grandmother has been choked and spit on and handcuffed. Why don't we instead dream up some motherfuckers who will set up the automatic renewal on our magazine subscriptions?

I've dated approximately one man who had to wear a tie

every day to work. And once I spent the night at his apartment and, after bolting upright in horror because homeboy had "space issues" and didn't like for me to fall asleep in his bed after sex, I ran into his kitchen and splashed some water on my face and then tried to make some coffee. Except I'd never used a French press before and I totally fucked the shit up, coffee grounds everyfuckingwhere, and then I burned him in the shower because I flushed the toilet while he was directly under the stream after I'd snuck in to pee in the first place. I was watching MTV in the living room at an obnoxious volume as he called and called my name, asking if I could pack him a lunch because he was running late. I didn't fucking do it because I was too busy watching Usher videos and attempting to emulate his sweet dance moves. Ten minutes later I was straining weak coffee through a sieve into a travel thermos and wrapping random leftovers in plastic wrap for his lunch (one bruised kiwi, a quarter of a dried-out rotisserie chicken, a handful of cashews, most of a brownie) while he grumbled in the bedroom. A box of new dress socks? No, I hadn't seen it. The bag from the dry cleaner with his pale blue shirt in it? Nope, can't remember which closet I'd hung it in. I was virtually useless. BUT . . .

I'd practiced tying a Windsor knot with the help of some YouTube videos and my roommate Joseph's least favorite tie, and I was ready. I was ready to redeem myself in the eyes of my go-to fantasy, I was ready to be that woman who wrapped her hair in a towel so that she could apply her makeup and fetch her man's tweed jacket from the cedar closet without dripping leave-in conditioner all over his nice carpet (because, of course, he owns this condo and this carpeting was so expensive and when I dropped that sloppy joe in the hallway last weekend he really did look like he was actually contemplating slitting my actual throat), and even though I was scared, I WAS READY. There was bitter, gritty coffee in a busted travel mug and a crumpled plastic Jewel bag on the counter containing the kind of lunch you wouldn't feed your worst enemy and he isn't going to marry me, but goddamn it I was going to tie the shit out of that tie even if it killed me. He was wearing cuff links, and a heady cloud of aftershave hung over the room, and he smiled when I asked if I could help with his tie and handed it over.

"Wide end on the right," I murmured to myself. "Cross the wide end over the narrow end, or is it the narrow end over the wide? Then bring the wide end up through the loop between the collar and the tie, no, wait, then bring the wide end back down?" I stepped back to survey my handiwork so far. My eyes widened in horror. "I'm just going to do this when I get to the office," he sighed, yanking loose the merit badge–worthy Boy Scout bowline knot I'd made from his necktie. He was so annoyed that he left his lunch on the counter. So I ate the brownie. And the kiwi. Okay, fine, I ate the whole fucking thing. Stress eating is a real thing.

I'm not going to have a baby. Not a biological one, at least, and that is a big deal to a lot of people. No, I have not done exhaustive research and I have not undergone extensive tests; I haven't harvested any eggs or thought about in vitro fertilization, because the first time I had that up-the-nose down-the-throat tube threaded UP MY NOSE and DOWN MY THROAT by a twelve-year-old medical student whose hands were shaking like a leaf during a torrential downpour while he reassured me that I should remain calm, I decided that whatever evil was brewing in the pit of my belly was never going to ever have to compete with a baby. A burrito? Probably, if I could ever stop shitting. Two gametes that would become a zygote that would then become a human life-form? Decidedly not. And that is a motherfucking deal breaker for a lot of these dudes.

A few years ago I was taking classes at community college because I hadn't quite yet given up all hope. There was a tall African dude with a deep, melodious voice in the class, and he was sexy. He carried a briefcase to community college, people: DUDE WAS OBVIOUSLY A WINNER. I spent the entire summer semester wondering when this asshole was going to ask me out on a goddamned date. Not kidding. Two and a half legit months making sure my hoodies were clean and my flip-flops weren't covered in street puke because I just *knew* that this dude was head over heels in love with me and was going to whisk me off to midlevel-management, associate-degree paradise. The last day of class I was in line turning in the final group project that only I had worked on, when he grabbed my hand and said, "Let's get a drink to celebrate the end of the term?" And that was incredibly romantic, but my dumb ass still had three more classes to sit through that afternoon (what the fuck . . . ?) and I didn't want to miss my African history final fucking around in a bar with my African future. I aced my multiple-choice final and met Frank at a bar near my apartment because I am lazy and I just don't feel like trying very hard anymore. He got a beer, I got a shot, and we spent half an hour making fun of most of our classmates, all total goddamned idiots. He was funny and smart and he wore polo shirts in earnest, and he even let me see what was inside his briefcase: bundles of paperwork from his job as a manager at Hollywood Video. "I love videos," I swooned, flagging down the bartender for another Jameson. He asked me about my job (it's the best) and my educational goals (none whatsoever) and then he asked if I wanted to have children. I felt the fear creeping up the back of my neck. "Today?" I asked, stalling. "It's kind of late in the day, don't you think?" OH, HA-HA-HA LOLZ.

Frank explained to me that having several strapping young sons to carry on his bloodline was the thing he wanted in life more than anything else and that adoption, or saving all that kid money to spend our golden years traveling abroad and trying not to die from a heart attack during sex, was totally out of the question. And then *I* explained to *him* that the only thing I planned on giving birth to in the near future was a roast beef sandwich with horseradish mayo and that fostering seventeen kids was pretty much the only reason I would ever want to get rich. "We wouldn't even need a maid, see?" I said, diagramming our adopted family on the back of a menu. "If we space out the ages just right, neither of us would have to wash a single dish, for like, the next thirty years. It's fucking genius. Also: CHILD ARMY." He signaled for the check.

"Can I still get a discount on my membership?" I asked as he politely handed the bartender his credit card. He rolled his eyes and nodded, digging a coupon out of his briefcase. I never did take that *Steel Magnolias* DVD back. Because fuck him.

I can't make pancakes. I feel like pancakes are these fundamental things that all good, husband-snagging women are capable of making. What is a Sunday morning for if not the sizzle of hotcakes on the griddle and bacon in the pan? What is that age-old tradition of "breakfast for dinner" if it doesn't include a fluffy stack of buttermilk silver dollars? There are lots of things I can cook, and there are a handful of things I make exceptionally well. But I have lived alone for a really long fucking time, long enough to be satisfied with a handful of microwaved Lit'l Smokies and a gluten-free cupcake for dinner. I made a big, fancy dinner a couple of weeks ago, mushroom bourguignon because I was going through a vegetarian cleanse thing, but don't worry, I'm over that brief bout of mental illness and eating so much sausage again. I spent an afternoon in my kitchen slicing and washing baby portabellas, making a roux and boiling wine and beef broth to make gravy, and when it was all done I got in bed and watched *The Mindy Project* on Hulu.

There are all of these recipes that I make and sometimes eat and I usually wish someone handsome was around to make sure they taste good, and someone who won't just eat the whole pot because he's spent half his paycheck on fancy spices to make it. But what if he doesn't want rogan josh or roasted skate wing? What if dude just wants a homemade apple pie?!

I cannot properly fold a fitted sheet. My whites often turn out dishwater gray. I have no household tips or tricks that involve apple cider vinegar. I needed to change that humidifier filter three months ago. And while these aren't the things someone notices upon making your acquaintance, I am way more scared of a dislocated button or a bee-stung appendage than I am a text that reads, "Where should we go for dinner?" That is the easy shit, the restaurant/the hot new bar/the spot with the best undiscovered rock band. I could write you a list of the best places to bat your eyelashes in a dimly lit room in the company of a dashing paramour, but if I needed to make an omelet for the hot naked body still wrapped in my sheets, I'd have no idea. This is why we need places that deliver breakfast. And why my next paycheck is going into my tooth-implant savings fund.

sorry i shit on your dick

Dear New Boyfriend,

Please buy decent toilet paper. Oh, I know. That Scott business is hella cheap. Plus there are one thousand sheets! It's such an amazing economical value! But it feels like coarse sandpaper on my butthole. Also, when I'm really trying to get my dirt star squeaky clean, that garbage disintegrates and leaves itchy crumbs that get caught in my ass hair. And I can't hang out at your place if I almost set my butthole on fire every time. And maybe you don't want me to hang out, which is cool. But don't you care even a little bit about your own little brown eye? Stop torturing it. Make your toilet life better. Spend the extra two bucks, you bastard.

Don't be weird if I almost shit in your car. It will happen. Not the shitting, necessarily, but guaranteed if you know me for more than an hour and a half at some point during our acquaintance I am going to grip my middle in a panic and turn desperately to you, begging you to PUT YOUR FOOT ON THE GOD-DAMNED GAS BECAUSE IF YOU DON'T YOU'LL BE CLEANING DIARRHEA OUT OF THE POROUS FABRIC ON YOUR CAR SEAT. Oh, I'm kidding. I'll clean it. But you will have to stand there watching me, and that is almost equally humiliating. So drive fast. And always be on the lookout for places with public restrooms. I might miss half the movie, but that's okay. And you don't have to feel weird because I spent three-quarters of the Drake concert indisposed. Enjoy that shit, bro. I only want to hear "The Resistance" anyway.

If I say, "I can't eat that," let that be the goddamned end of it. No, I'm not on a diet. (YES, I should be, but that is a discussion to be had another day.) My Crohn's usually flares from stress. And what a pain in the dick that is because it means I can never just, say, avoid cheese and have that be the end of it. It's not that simple. Sometimes I can have meat and sometimes that same meat makes my gut feel like it's eating itself from the inside. So if I'm having a bad day, and I turn my nose up at that plate of pork belly tacos, don't be salty. YOU KNOW I WANT THAT SHIT. It's just that today is a bread-and-white-rice day. So quit rubbing those carnitas all in my face. Unless it's part of some sex thing, in which case: by all means.

Visit me in the fucking hospital. Guaranteed it's harder for me than it is for you. Seriously, I promise you that it is. And I know it's not fun, but there's cable TV and all the apple juice and unsalted vegetable broth you can drink. Bring me some magazines, please. And an iPhone charger. And some pajama bottoms if you have time to swing by my crib. Walking around with my ass out is the fucking worst. I'm a really fun patient. Seriously, I get all the good drugs and that makes me as sweet as a kitten. I promise I will be really happy to see you.

Adjust, sexually. This peripheral arthritis is a sonofabitch. So we're not doing that one position you saw in that porn you watched a couple of nights ago. My joints don't bend like that. This brace I have to wear on my left hand at night is uncomfortable, so please pretend you don't notice it if I happen to graze your taint with the edge of it. I swear it isn't intentional. If you stick your thumb in my asshole again I am probably going to shit on your dick. So don't do that. My bowels are hella unpredictable. You have to order anal sex two days in advance, like Peking duck. Try not to thrust so hard that it feels like you're boring a hole through my diaphragm, because sometimes I can't tell when this is pleasure pain or emergency pain. Be careful with my left knee. My right ankle joint is sore today. Man, this acid reflux is really making me want to die. I know, I know, why did we even bother with trying to fuck, anyway? This is why I'm exceptionally good at giving head. Next time, let's just do that. I might vomit on your balls, but that's not so bad. You can keep a shirt on.

Love,
Samantha

*how to get your disgusting
meat carcass ready for some new, hot sex*

I. BUY A CAN OF BARBASOL.

Chin whiskers are a real fucking thing, sister. I stopped taking birth control a year ago, because every time I turned the
goddamned television on there was another ad reminding me
that my old ass was going to have a heart attack or develop a
blood clot, and frankly, I don't have enough sex to warrant taking that kind of risk. And I'm the kind of asshole who would
ignore the throbbing pain traveling up my leg as a clot slowly
migrated upward to explode in my lungs because I was too busy
Instagramming pictures of my stupid dinner. I have an amazing
relationship with my gynecologist due to the winning combination of my childlike need to be shocking and provocative and

his infinite patience with a petulant toddler who is constantly barraging him with dumb-ass questions.

Two years ago, after he finished scraping barnacles off the sides of my underused cervix, he sat me down in the Serious Chair and asked if I had any concerns about my vagina health. That probably would have been a good time to confess that my irregular periods and occasional spotting hadn't cleared up, or I could've mentioned that the Metronidazole suppositories he regularly prescribed made my meathole smell like chemicals and bacon, but I DID NOT. Instead, I said, "I'm thinking about having sex with a woman. If I have a hangnail, and she's on her period, can my fingers get HIV?" So I was joking, because I paid attention in high school health class and I am not a total fucking idiot, but he looked at me soberly and proceeded to give me a detailed explanation of the ways blood-borne diseases can be transmitted, complete with a demonstration of how to properly outfit one's hand in a snug rubber glove prior to engaging in a hearty round of fingerbanging. I took notes on the back of one of those "Freeze your eggs!" pamphlets and made a mental note to never fuck around with this dude ever again. He didn't have time for my bullshit. But I just couldn't resist, so I said, "What if I have a cut on my gums?" and I'll let you figure out which lecture I got next.

Last year, on my thirty-second birthday, I sat at the end of the exam table, each of my naked breasts balanced heavily in either of the doctor's hands, and I said, "Listen. Let's stop pretending I'm ever going to have sex again before I go through early menopause. Can I stop taking birth control or what?" He gave me the "What the fuck do I care?" face and started talking to me about IUDs, and I was like, "Naw, son. How bad would it be if I just didn't ingest or insert a goddamned thing? Those commercials are downright terrifying, and I dance too hard to worry about an IUD shaking loose." (That is not a real thing that can happen, because science.) Then he did the breast exam, which makes me so uncomfortable I start to sweat every single time, and shamed me for not performing my own at home.

The last time I'd done one, lying on my back with my shirt off and my arm slung over my head just like the diagram I found on the Internet showed me, I was pressing and pressing and pressing my boobs in a circular motion until I happened upon a hard little knot in my armpit. I made an appointment right away, convinced that I had found some stage four malignancy that was *obviously* leeching into my lymph nodes and vital organs as the clock in the waiting room ticked backward, taunting me. After spending an eternity wedged into a tiny chair pretending to be interested in *People* while MY LIFE WAS SLIPPING THROUGH MY FINGERS (sob!) I was led back to a familiar exam room and ripped my shirt off to show the incredulous nurse my pulsating deathboil of doom. She squinted and poked at the nodule before excusing herself to get the doctor.

I started thinking about how best to update my Facebook with the tragic news. Should I be funny? Plead for sympathy? HOW DOES ONE MAKE A CANCER STATUS UPDATE?!

Chemo would be brutal, but I would handle it with grace, of course. I've always been incredibly fond of headscarves. The doctor let himself in without knocking and peered at my underarm, then he poked the bump a couple of times and rolled his eyes at me. He squeezed it, and a little dribble of rotten cheese oozed out onto his finger.

"Ingrown hair," he diagnosed.

"So, what, no radiation?" I asked.

"Warm compress, keep it clean, get out of my office."

And that was the end of my medical career.

That thoughtless jerk didn't warn me that my goddamned chin was going to turn into the back of a porcupine, though. Is this the shit that synthetic estrogen was saving me from?! Waking up to a motherfucking five o'clock shadow? Two months off the pill and I started to wonder whether a possible deathclot was worth it. Are you baby birds too young to have plucked your bristly neck folds yet? Well, let me tell you what that feels like: ABSOLUTELY HORRIBLE. Every morning I take that fancy Tweezerman *Elle* magazine encouraged me to buy and, instead of using it as intended, to artfully sculpt a supermodel eyebrow out of the coarse, unruly hair sprouting just below my hairline, I jut my lower jaw out as close to the vanity mirror as I can get it and grunt while yanking resistant hairs out of MY FUCKING FACE.

What cruel torment this aging is. Good thing I've found a way to beat it. Okay, no I haven't. I can literally step on my own nipples. BUT . . . I've discovered that if you (1) buy Barbasol instead of those fruity lady foams, and (2) buy disposable men's razors, you will feel much less like a dumb asshole when trying to get rid of your little granny beard every morning in the shower. They cost less, work more effectively, and won't leave proof of your grossness all over your nicked-up turkey waddle. Will you feel like a dude? Probably. But will your legs be hella smooth for a fraction of the cost?! Definitely. And believe me, I like all those cocoa butter strips and shit, too! But the first time I had to explain the long red scratch on my jaw to my boss was the last. What a beast.

2. SHOULD I WAX MY FUCKING ASSHOLE?

How bad do you guys let it get, between sexcapades? We're all friends here, right? So be honest: How far do you let yourself go? Okay, I'll go first: the minute I get dumped—well, after I make the voodoo doll from all the bits of hair I pulled out of the drain and scraps of fabric I've inconspicuously cut from all his shirts—I basically go through my bathroom with a garbage bag and throw out all the torture tools I used on myself throughout this most recent courtship. Out go all the pink-bottled depilatories and at-home wax kits and smelly under-eye creams so that I can swap in their less sexy counterparts that were hidden in the back of the hall closet every time dude spent the night at my crib: the utilitarian bottles of dandruff shampoo and dirt-scented body washes from Whole Foods.

This is not to say that I don't care about myself when I'm not seeing someone, because I *totally do*. I *only* buy myself the fanciest artisanal cheeses and the most expensive organic lip glosses my hourly wages can afford. I *never* buy clothes that have been worn by anyone else; I always take cabs, even if the distance traveled is ridiculously short; and I *only* purchase name-brand items, especially when the brand totally doesn't matter: Ziploc bags, Bounty paper towels, Tide laundry detergent. You get it: I'm good to me. And, thankfully, I have the lowest possible standards when it comes to acceptable maintenance of this feeble pre-corpse. The only hair that grosses me out is the hair on my forearms, and that's just because I paid a billion dollars for these shitty biker tattoos and I will be *damned* if your view of them is going to be obscured by wanton tufts of gorilla fur. I don't even mind that coarse toe hair until summer comes around, and that's because I'm a disgusting hippie who refuses to keep closed-toe shoes on her feet if the temperature rises even one degree above fifty.

Not that I shave all that much to begin with. "Bohemian" is still a thing a smelly, dirty person can reasonably claim to be, yes? But when I suspect someone is going to see my stubbled flesh in a dimly lit bedroom, I do have the decency to run the Epilady over my meaty calves and use exfoliating salt scrub on the chicken skin that covers my elbows. AND ON SPECIAL OCCASIONS I PULL OUT THE BEARD TRIMMER.

The woman at Sally Beauty had eyed me skeptically as I pretended to read the labels on the industrial-size bottles of hair relaxer and crystal gel. After a horrific experience with a bikini waxer (blood, sweat, tears, SHIT ON THE TABLE) I vowed to never again expose my tender booty cheese to a bitch armed with a bag of fabric strips and a vat of bubbling hot wax, but I was about to have a third date with a hot dude who *would not* shutthefuckup about how much he absolutely *loves* eating pussy. OH, BORING. I mean, I don't really love being eaten out. As a matter of fact, I'm downright ambivalent about lying on my back for half an hour trying to clench my butthole shut and concentrate on my happy place while homeboy fruitlessly gnashes his teeth against all my healthy bacteria. Despite my disdain I let them do it anyway, because feminism. And the very least I can do to be of assistance, other than not eating a ton of beans and raw spinach for a couple of days prior, is take a wacker to my ladyweeds. But that Brazilian shit is for suckers.

My sister asked why I didn't just trim it myself. "Like, with scissors?" I asked, shuddering at the mental image of me balanced precariously with one foot on the edge of the tub while attacking my labia majora with a pair of pinking shears. "No, stupid," she replied, incredulous. "With a pair of clippers. Clippers with a fucking safety guard. So you don't shred your labia into a hundred pieces." This, of course, had never before occurred to me. And so off I went to the beauty supply store. A prolonged, sheepish game of cat and mouse ensued, during which I pretended that I was buying a beard trimmer for my hirsute imaginary boyfriend—"Is this the kind of thing he can use in his nose?"—while she rolled her eyes and reluctantly played along.

The first time I used it I was so terrified of either electrocuting myself or hacking my vulva into a million little pieces that I dialed 911 on my cell phone and set it on the edge of the sink within easy reach in case I needed to press the call button. I am more confident now, but I still am too shy and uneasy to use a mirror so (from what I can feel, blindly groping around in my dry, empty bathtub) I still end up with a pubic lawn that looks like a child mowed it. IN THE DARK. The hair doesn't really bother me all that much, but one time this dude told me that fucking a full bush is like sticking his dick into a Brillo pad. And then I sat there, in his bed, and watched him pantomime what fucking a Brillo pad would feel like. It is an image that has stuck with me: my coarse ladyhair sloughing the skin off some unsuspecting penis. So now, if I like a dude, I show him by scorching my earth so I don't shred his dick like cheese in a box grater. (Picture that in real life. It's hilarious.)

3. MANI VERSUS PEDI

You may have one or the other, sir, but not both. Both escalates the game to a level that no man can reasonably be expected to achieve. Especially if it's winter and I have to struggle out of my snow boots and hike up the stiff legs of my salt-encrusted jeans just to get the shit done.

The first time I got my toes sucked it was a goddamned revelation. I didn't know that it was something I even wanted until it was happening, until Daniel was at the foot of his bed dressed only in his stylish black boxer briefs, cupping my heel in his hand while gently biting my baby toe between his teeth. My first thought: "THIS IS WEIRD." Second thought: "I have been wearing flip-flops all day. In the rain. There is homeless person urine on the sole of that disgusting foot." He moved from one toe to the next, lips/tongue/teeth, the whole thing, and even though I'd blurted, "You're going to catch the flu!" as he kissed the chipped red polish on my big toe, his determination remained unwavering. Daniel is one of these dudes who, like, worships every stretch mark and makes sweet, incandescent love to each and every misshapen precancerous mole. The first time we had sex I was on my period. And not day-seven-a-few-spots-here-and-there period, but day-three-heavy-flow-bleeding-like-a-stuck-pig period. What a fucking soldier.

So when he went for my foot, I wasn't surprised. He was the first dude who had ever asked me to slip my finger in his asshole to locate his prostate, the first dude to put his tongue in inappropriate places, the first dude who seemed happy to get up from a roll in the hay that left him looking like he'd just survived a car crash. I still don't know what he got out of it; maybe there's some erogenous zone on the tongue that responds well to the rough, calloused skin on the side of my big toe, but I didn't even care. It feels good, like walking barefoot in squishy wet sand with warm water lapping at your toes. I had never before paid much attention to my feet other than the occasional salt scrub at the end of a hot shower.

I couldn't just ask one of my asshole friends what the proper protocol was prior to performing a tonsil exam with my phalanges, so instead I made an appointment to have a pedicure because I'd watched enough episodes of *Sex and the City* that it seemed like the right thing to do. And I know it's not a big deal and it's not a rite of passage and that something that costs $22 should not be the cause of such internal hand-wringing, but I am uncomfortable having someone sit below me digging street detritus from my nail beds while I flip through Kirstie Alley's before and after pictures in *People*. Especially when I can awkwardly cut my own jagged toenails over the toilet without fear of hush-toned nail technician reprisal. But I did it. I suffered through dozens of squirmy, restless pedicures so that this fine young gentleman could insert a perfectly square cherry-red toenail into his mouth at regular intervals.

I hate those weird, slippery chairs. I hate trying to balance my heel on the footrest while the opposite knee is dangerously close to dislocating my bottom jaw. I hate choosing from forty-seven identical shades of red polish on the wall. Those chairs make my stomach hurt, and then I feel like I have to shit, and then I start sweating because I feel like I have to shit, and then I have to try not to slip and risk either breaking my ankle or kicking this bitch in the chin all while clenching my unwaxed asshole because twenty-plus minutes with my knees pressed to my chest means OH MY GOD, I HAVE TO SHIT. Have you ever tried to mask the sound of stress diarrhea in a tiny nail shop bathroom, surrounded by the prying eyes of a hundred little Buddha statues and clusters of dusty silk flowers? My deepest sympathies to you if you have. That hand soap is always so fucking drying.

Which is hella noticeable considering that my hands feel like they've been tenderized and run through a dishwasher cycle. I bleed every time. Every single motherfucking time. They start pushing skin back and snipping at my cuticles and inevitably, without fucking fail, I start leaking blood down my hands. Then comes the obligatory lecture about how it's my fault because I don't moisturize enough, lest I balk at shelling out twelve bucks for butchered hands. But even if I rubbed Crisco into these softball mitts every night before bed that wouldn't counteract being hacked to bits by a woman who is actively gossiping in her native tongue, picking deviled ham from under my fingernails, and watching daytime television at the same time. It's the reason I keep Band-Aids in my purse.

And that, in a nutshell, is why you can either get ten perfectly shaved-down little piggies or you can get two paraffin-dipped meat hooks dripping a bloody cuticle trail in my wake but, no, sir, you cannot, you WILL NOT, get them both.

4. LINGERIE IS GROSS.

I love a hot bra. There is nothing on earth sexier than a hot goddamned bra. And I have good-size tits, so buying hot bras is totally rewarding, provided that I don't have to wear a padded plunging sweetheart during the workday or run from a burglar in a lacy French-cut demi. Because I would knock out my own front teeth. My real-life, riding-the-train, shoveling-shit-for-twelve-hours-a-day bras are essentially made of black box material. They're sexy, I guess, especially when they're packed full of breast meat, but no one wants to undo three unforgiving layers of heavy corsetry only to then be faced with five menacing hooks and harness-like straps. I buy these towering feats of construction, Cacique smooth-satin full-coverage bras, for no less than $3,712 apiece, and they are WORTH EVERY PENNY. I'm not going to run a marathon in one or anything, but they keep my nipples from getting caught in my waistband, and for that I would give up everything.

But nobody wants to fuck someone wearing his mama's house bra, even if it's hot pink, so when I think a date is going to end in some second-base action, I prep by unearthing my frilly little things, wash them by hand in Woolite, then dry them in the salad spinner. Can you even comprehend the work that goes into all this? And it doesn't even guarantee an orgasm! But I gotta do it, because MOM BRA. PS, never eat salad at my fucking house.

5. PUSH-UPS, KEGELS, YOGA STRETCHES

I try not to have sex on the first date if I can help it. When I was younger there wouldn't be these epic lapses between sexual encounters but, considering that I am currently in month six of a vaginal drought, nowadays I have to get myself back into fighting shape when faced with the possibility of some brand-new sex. The first time is always the worst time, because even if you both are just TOTALLY FUCKING DYING to get your tongues on each other, shit is always going to be a little awkward. There's going to be some fumbling, some kissing too hard (or not hard enough), some offbeat sex rhythm, some mismatching of your bodies' puzzle pieces. But that's the buttery shit about getting to bang someone new, right? The teaching someone new what you like and how you like it? The discovery of someone else's erogenous zones? The masking of your horror when you find out this motherfucker is into that crazy-ass shit you read about on the Internet?!

Here's what sucks, though: for a generally out-of-shape person, I like to be in decent "sex shape," and sitting around drinking my feelings (emotions are just chemicals, emotions are just chemicals) for six months isn't necessarily the best way. All my banging muscles have atrophied, bro. My legs can't spread that wide! My side cramps if I have to stay in this position too long! WHAT THE FUCK ARE YOU TRYING TO DO WITH MY KNEES?! So, to save myself some unnecessary embarrassment, I came up with the following lazy sex-specific workout program.

1. Give better hand jobs. I keep a set of twelve-pound dumbbells in my hall closet. After a good first date, I start doing biceps curls and triceps extensions while I watch television or talk on the phone in anticipation of the day I'm going to have to hold this meaty pre-corpse up during some butt sex. Then when I'm tired I lie on my back and do presses with them to strengthen my pectorals. I also stretch my wrists a lot. And I drink water, because sweating through an hour of *Top Model* cycle 172 while working out your shoulder muscles is exhausting. Also, health.

2. Try not to pee. This one is good for the bus stop or train platform, especially early in the morning after you've had your coffee. Get up, do your morning ritual, pee in the shower or wherever, eat your Bran O's or your Flax Chex or whatever fiber-rich cereal your physician guilted you into eating, and your coffee/juice/double

whiskey neat with a water back and beer chaser. Get dressed, begin commute. Halfway to the train you're probably going to have to pee. Shit, too, depending on your constitution. Now hold your ladymuscles taut and don't ruin those leggings you are trying to pass off as pants. That's right, SQUEEZE. Keep squeezing, even as that old lady with the collapsible shopping cart refuses to collapse that goddamned shopping cart and so instead jabs you in the thigh with it. Keep squeezing, despite the fact that those teenagers are actively waving guns around your head and listening to their music out loud even though you can fucking see the headphones draped around their necks. Keep squeezing, even though that woman from HR that you hate ties up the bathroom for twenty minutes at the start of every workday. Three days of that and you'll be able to circumcise a dude all by yourself. Without a scalpel.

3. Fatnastics. My Achilles tendons are the worst. A few years ago I busted my foot running through Edgewater at two in the morning on a Sunday wearing flip-flops and club clothes, and these shits ain't been right ever since. I have flat feet and heel spurs and I already told you how I feel about pedicures, bro. But I can't be getting leg and feet cramps in the middle of the coitus. It's happened, and every time I have to push some mouth-breathing Neanderthal off me to hobble painfully to the kitchen in hopes of scoring a still-ripe banana, I nearly die of embarrassment in the process. So rather than suffer through that nightmare I instead implement a succession of calf and thigh and foot stretches into my daily routine. Since it isn't real, I can't describe the shit,

but just imagine a lot of awkward toe touching and foot flexing until the cat starts making me uncomfortable with her snickering.

READY, SET, gross and awkward and humiliating even though I tried to prep for it, FUCK.

massive wet asses

All I ever want to know about is how other people have sex. I'm so nosy and gross. I want to know exactly what they do: how long they kiss for, if he has to beg her to go down on him, the whole thing. Who initiates it? Has she ever accidentally peed in his mouth? Does he let her stick a finger in his asshole? When I meet a couple, first I admire their handsome outerwear (I mean, right? Isn't that how you do it when you're angling to make a good impression?) And then I wonder, like, if he has to ask her permission before he rolls over onto her in the middle of the night. You know, how does the sex bargaining work? Does he do that "cuddle cuddle spooning, whoa I have an erection" sneak attack? Or does he just compliment the shit out of that broad until her panties fucking simply evaporate? Which of these gentlemen is the top? Are these girls into tribbing? Which one does the penis stuff?!

It's not even really that perverted; I have a genuine intellectual curiosity about how other people get down. I have never been banging anyone long and/or consistently enough to create a pattern: chicken wings on Tuesday, sex on Wednesday, *American Idol* on Thursday, take the dry cleaning Friday, blow job Saturday, etc. All my boyfriends have been "once-a-week dinner and drinks / maybe a movie / spend the night at his place" kind of boyfriends. I'd have no idea what on earth to do if I slept next to the same warm body for more than three nights in a row. That is literally something that has *never* happened to me. And I'm thirty-two years old! All you jerks complaining on Facebook that your boyfriend of five years forgot to take the garbage out one fucking time and I haven't even spent a Memorial Day weekend with a dude?! Shut the fuck up and die, please.

Anyway, this is the type of thing that consumes me, this wondering if people have a code word or gesture or something that says, "Tonight, my love, I am going to put it in your butthole. It will be spectacular. You will thoroughly enjoy it." When all of your relationships are over before anyone has had a birthday or any major holidays have occurred, bitches ain't really gotta worry about the whole "asking for sex" part. It is assumed, naturally, that since I haven't seen you in two weeks, and you sent a sort of ambivalent mean-ass text yesterday, and I ordered and drank an entire bottle of French wine at dinner, that once we get back to my place I expect you to eat me out while pretending to like it while I pretend you are good at it. And then I will jack you off, probably get a leg cramp, try not to fart on your nuts because I ate all that cheese at the restaurant, use my LELO on the toilet after you pass out because you're a total dick who doesn't give a shit about my sexual needs, and then, after tiptoe-ing back into the bedroom in an attempt not to wake you up, I will try to sleep with that painful mattress seam digging into my soft meat and the side of my face because I'm not strong enough to haul your sleeping carcass off my side of the goddamned bed. Can't we just make holding hands while partially clothed a real motherfucking thing? Is mutual masturbation really so terrible? Because actual human sex is sometimes the goddamned worst.

The first pornographic film I ever purchased was a towering cinematic achievement entitled *Massive Wet Asses*. The year was 2006, and I was twenty-five years old. An avid masturbator, I had grown bored with my imagination's ability to come up with new ways for Tom Cruise and Method Man to fuck me. So I went to the porn store. Tucked neatly into the small but decently appointed black-on-black category within Cupid's Treasures' hard-core DVD section, this visual masterpiece not only bore a cover with images that looked like stills from a low-budget rap video (buff, shirtless gentlemen heavily laden with platinum rope chains; ample-bottomed, scantily clad women whose glistening haunches appeared to have been coated liberally with Italian salad dressing), but *also* promised an action-packed ninety minutes full of "fine-ass sluts with massive wet butts," and "phat-ass chicks hungry for big thick dicks." I felt a little guilty that it was only going to cost me $29.99. That much "monster cock slipping and sliding on a massive ride" was easily worth twice the asking price. (Current retail price: $3.85, expedited shipping available.) I also bought my very first vibrator that day, a nondescript lavender sheath that had three settings and required two D batteries. Bat-teries that—*quelle* surprise—could be purchased for nearly twice what I would've paid for them at Walgreens behind the counter during checkout. One-stop dick shop.

· · · · ·

Of course I had seen dirty movies before, but we're talking the basics, at best. Elementary-level solo sex material. Friday-night premium cable soft-core, teeming with waxed Barbie dolls and their synthetic blond hair built like broomsticks with water balloons affixed to their chests. I figured if that's what I had to look like in order for a man to get an erection in my presence then I was never, ever, ever going to have sex in my whole fucking life. It was too depressing to even masturbate to, so I'd just put my headphones on and do my geography homework while watching *Emmanuelle*. One of the vaginas in my house had hidden a couple of issues of *Playgirl* in her room, but a fruity photo spread of a naked dude reclining on a table littered with rose petals and lit candles with his genitals wrapped around the deed to a house in the suburbs wasn't really my style. And left to its own devices, my sluggish fantasy brain is totally lazy and downright unimaginative when it comes to providing suitable autoerotic mental stimulation, recycling variations on the same two themes: clean-shaven, broad-shouldered men in sharply cut suits paying for a steak dinner in a fancy restaurant with their credit cards and not expecting a blow job in return, or heavily bearded, broad-shouldered men slaughtering bison with their bare hands before butchering it and bringing it home, cooking it in butter, and serving it to me in bed without expecting anal sex as payment. My brain is apparently singularly focused. On dinner. And possibly anal sex.

On the train ride home I was 100 percent convinced that everyone knew the opaque black bag shoved in the pocket of my hoodie had come from the sex store, and it made me feel sexy in a perverted, creepy way. My roommate at the time had left town for the weekend, and I'm pretty sure I stopped at Dinkel's to get a box of cupcakes before ordering a pizza when I got home, and that I spent the entirety of that weekend without any pants on, vanilla cake crumbs scattered between my sweaty sheets. Sure, I'd had plenty of sex by that point, but what the fuck is "sex" when you're twenty-two other than mindless bouncing up and down on top of, or sliding awkwardly back and forth beneath, an inarticulate Neanderthal who has no idea about clitoral stimulation? Besides, I was more interested in things like making my phone ring. Gosh, it was of such crucial importance to me to have a man actually pick up the phone and dial my number back then, even if he didn't really say anything interesting once I'd answered. And having someone around to shave my legs for, because, to this day, I don't unless I'm guaranteed someone handsome is going to see them.

Masturbating heretofore had involved so many minutes of intense concentration on both the fantasy in my head and whatever my hand was doing, and that shit would sometimes take a goddamned half an hour. Really, bitches, who has that kind of time? Plus, it makes my hand joints sore. Right now I probably have $6,297,431 worth of vibrators in my pajama drawer. No more $15 plastic dicks, these days I have a collection of fancy silicone LELOs and Jimmyjanes and Fun Factorys that are curved for the G-spot and flared for the butthole and waterproof for the bathroom. I work fifty hours a week, dude. I can't stagger through the door after a bone-crushing day and lube up my fingers while imagining Jon Hamm's voice in my ear for forty-five minutes. I want to slip my Extase Liberté in while eating my dinner over the kitchen sink and looking at pictures of dudes kissing on my phone, have an orgasm, wash my plate (eh, maybe I'll do it tomorrow), then take my ass to bed.

· · · · ·

Porn pretty much saved my life. *Finally* there was this magical celluloid place into which I could escape and watch other
people fucking like wild animals and spitting on each other and
eating out each other's asses and, with the help of that cheap
piece of plastic that rattled like a lawn mower, in approximately
thirty-five seconds my entire worldview would be completely
changed. I'd go from a bad day to a good one, from feeling
terrible about myself to thinking I was totally fucking sexy and
desirable. I didn't ever stop. I JUST COULDN'T. And you better be glad I didn't, because eventually I would have opened
fire in a grocery store or some shit. You're alive today because I
learned how to reach my own G-spot while watching a woman
get pissed on for rent money. And, thanks to *Massive Wet Asses*
in particular, I understood that this wagon I'm dragging isn't
something to be ashamed of, this massive dry ass is actually
appealing to a small subset of grown men who live at home with
their cuckold mothers and *also* are recent parolees.

And porn continues to be a savior for my weary vagina. I
know some women have a problem with a dude beating off to
cream pies on the Internets all day, but, girl: THAT'S JUST
YOU. Here's the thing about porn, computer or otherwise: if
a dude expected me to have sex with him as often as he would
like to have sex with me (taking into consideration the fountain
of smoldering desire that represents, of course), or as often as he
thinks about having sex with passersby on the street, or as often
as he urinates and the handling of his dick reminds him of sex,
or as often as a strong gust of wind grazes his cock and reminds
him just how much he loves sex, my vagina would be nothing
more than a swollen mound of bruised, rancid hamburger meat

beaten bloody and raw by the incessant rabbit-fucking of a dude who has reduced my importance in his life to that of a talking blow-up doll. I'd become nothing more than a collection of orifices into which he might repeatedly jab his erection. And, considering the conversational skills of the average adult male, that might be preferable to actually letting one talk to me about things he thinks are important; EXCEPT, I have to go to work and shit. And rather than try to explain to my boss that I'm wearing a head bandage today because my manfriend ear-fucked the shit out of me last night, why not just let that guy beat off to tenish lusty minutes of some hot broad on a Sybian?! I have stuff to do, mang.

AND, SINCE I *KNOW* YOU WERE WONDERING, THIS IS HOW I HAVE SEX

1. By this point of the whole operation, I'm usually pretty tired. Not gonna lie, I'm usually hoping dude has fallen asleep on the couch after waiting for twenty minutes while I washed my asshole in his sink. But if he's still awake, I will rally. I mean, if I *have* to. Some of these jerks won't just settle for a goddamned blow job.

2. I like to talk to my partner about sex like I'm closing a business deal. Super formal, lots of fine print, the mentioning of "synergy," and a firm handshake. I negotiate the leaving on of as many of my clothes as possible. "Really, dude, I fuck better with a T-shirt on." And set a timer: "Fifteen minutes, then we are watching *The Voice*. Do we understand each other?" Then the intercourse begins. "You may enter me." Usually they just

stand there dumbfounded, satisfied to sign whatever contract placed in front of them provided that my pants are still coming off.

3. OH SNAP, FOREPLAY. Ladies will be mad as hell if I don't list the one reason we even RSVP'd to the pussy party. I don't know how the rest of you assholes get down but, for me, foreplay consists of standing outside waiting for the bed to be strewn with rose petals as the string quartet warms up. I like to be blindfolded and gently guided into the boudoir, then nestled into silk pillows just as a choir of angels descends from the heavens sweetly singing my name. Just kidding, bitch. I, like the rest of you, very much enjoy standing awkwardly in the corner of an unfamiliar bedroom hoping that something darker than pitch-black will be invented in the time it takes me to get my jeans unzipped and down around my ankles. I also appreciate the delicate art of trying to kiss someone with my mouth open without disgustingly licking the inside of his nostril while trying to get all four clasps on my industrial-strength bra undone at the same time. Then I gotta massage those shoulder grooves caused by my huge tits for a second, trying to smooth that shit out before dude notices that they are deep enough to swim in. Rush through some sort of hand- / blow- /foot-job activity so that I can get to the part where having a blanket over me doesn't seem out of place.

4. Stick a finger up my birth canal to make sure I won't get rug burn when this insensitive asshole starts jackhammering my chocha.

5. Under the covers, talking dirty, making uncomfortable

jokes to deflect from my body hatred, pretending to know what "tightening my Kegel muscles" means and trying to do whatever the fuck that is. PUT YOUR FINGER RIGHT THERE FOR THREE MINUTES WHILE BITING ME OVER HERE NO A LITTLE FASTER PLEASE A LITTLE HARDER KEEP THE PRESSURE RIGHT THERE WAIT DON'T STOP TWO MORE SECONDS OKAY DONE GOOD NIGHT.

6. Or sometimes I like to scroll through Tumblr girl-on-girl porn on my phone with my hand in my pants while dude plays *Madden NFL 13*. Trust me. Just as good.

dinner on the couch

· ·

When someone is coming over (read: when I'm sitting at home alone but want to pretend I care about myself) the first thing I like to do is light a coffee-scented candle, so that at the very least there is the *illusion* of warmth and food. I never got into coffee for the same reasons I never really got into wine: it seems unnecessarily fussy and complicated, getting good at it feels cost-prohibitive, and the results are fair to middling at best. I enjoy that thick, warm sleepiness that rapidly pouring a liter of wine into an empty stomach provides as much as anyone, but it feels just as good when that wine costs six dollars as it does when the wine costs fourteen. Or twenty-seven. As much as a meal at a decent restaurant, or as much as my gas bill in the winter months. The candle makes things cozy and that special food issue of *Kinfolk* casually tossed on the floor at the foot of the bed shows that I care about food but I don't *care* care about it.

I had dinner with some friends the other night, and these friends are, like, lawyers and professors I met late enough in life that they've never had to borrow five bucks from me or sleep on my couch for a week, and one of them ordered wine by the region and upon first sip pronounced it "complex and multidimensional" and here is my fucking train of thought while those words were coming out of her mouth as I silently drained my "cheapest gin you got" over ice with a splash of diet tonic:

"Is she talking about the wine?"

"Could I have been chewing the last piece of sourdough in the bread basket so loudly that I missed the change of conversation?"

"What, does this wine read the Sunday paper and refer to movies as films?"

"I have no idea where wine even comes from."

"Do you have to take some kind of wine class in finishing school?"

"What would that sentence sound like if I said it, and could I say it without laughing?"

"I wish wine tasted more like grape juice."

"I am too stupid to be at this dinner."

"Ha-ha, I'm pretty funny—that films line was a good one."

And then the food came out and there were sauce dots and spit foams, and my fraudulent ass was sitting there wondering what the rules are about asking a cabdriver to hit the drive-thru. I don't care what makes anyone happy—I enjoy watching Triple H's WWE entrance montages on YouTube—I mean, what authority do I have to criticize anyone's choices ever? But I literally have no idea what to do when I am served part of my dinner balanced precariously on a spoon and that ounce of squid toast costs as much as a night at the movies. That is money that could have been better spent on a vanilla diffuser to trick anyone who stops by that I might be baking when really I haven't bought eggs in more than six months.

HOW I LIKE TO EAT PASTA
WHEN I AM JUST CHILLING BY MYSELF

Ingredients
> a box of whatever pasta shape you enjoy
> 1 pint of grape tomatoes (I hate big, mealy tomatoes, ugh)
> olive oil
> a tube of minced garlic (in the produce section)
> dried basil

dried oregano

crushed red pepper

sea salt and fresh black pepper (I'm just trying to be cute;
    you can use regular pepper, duh.)

shaved Parmesan (THIS MAKES A DIFFERENCE,
    TRUST.)

Listen, you've probably already heard this story, but I don't care—I'm telling it again: I once dated a grown man with a college degree who told me that he only ate angel-hair pasta. And I'm no snob—I mean, shit, I eat microwave pizza rolls—but this gentleman was turning down a home-cooked meal because he either (1) did not approve of the shape of my pasta, or (2) did not understand that no matter how it looks, it is all eggs and semolina. I stood in my kitchen, glasses fogged by the steam wafting up from the walnut pesto bowtie pasta I wasted an afternoon to prepare, only to have my offering rejected by a talking grizzly bear in overpriced athletic footwear. Anyway, I like to make this with slightly undercooked spaghetti, but you do what feels good to you.

1. Boil some salted water, then cook the pasta however long the box says. I like to shave a minute or two off the cooking time depending on the pasta type and immediately rinse it in cold water because gooey, sticky pasta makes me want to die.

2. Heat up a little drizzle or two of the olive oil in a saucepan on medium heat, then squeeze in however much garlic suits you. I like a tablespoon or more, but I'm gross.

3. At some point before now you should have cut all the grape tomatoes in half the long way. If not, take the gar-

lic and oil off the stove and slice the tomatoes. Dump
them into the warm garlic slurry and keep the heat on
medium-high, stirring with a wooden spoon and kinda
gently mashing them so their liquidy insides glug out.

4. This doesn't sound appealing, I know, but it'll get all
   fragrant and saucy and you won't be grossed out. Add
   a pinch of basil and a pinch of oregano, like a literal
   pinch of each, then shake some crushed red pepper in
   there and a couple of pinches of salt and a few grinds of
   pepper. Taste it before going too ham with the spices,
   okay? You know how salty you like things; you don't
   need me to tell you to start with ⅛ teaspoon of salt at a
   time and keep adding until you get it where you want
   it; you're a grown-up! You know how to salt!

5. But in case you don't, an eighth is as good a place as any
   to start.

6. This should be a quick process. I mean, the point of
   getting in bed at 7:00 p.m. with a bowl of food is that
   you don't want to labor over it all goddamn night; you
   want to walk in the door, pull your bra off through your
   shirtsleeve in one swift motion, and be eating while
   bathed in the phosphorescent blue glow of the television half an hour later, maximum. Sometimes I order
   delivery before I even finish working so that my lamb
   biryani gets to my door at the same time I do and I can
   start ripping pieces off the garlic naan as soon as the
   elevator door shuts. So heap a pile of your cooked pasta
   into the biggest bowl you own, spoon enough of the

hot tomato mixture over it to lightly coat it, toss, then sprinkle it with shaved Parmesan.

6.5 That powdery Parmesan in a can is fine if that's what you're into but not here. This doesn't taste good covered in cheese dust; you want to swirl your noodles in spicy tomato oil, then stab into a sheet of salty, tangy Parmesan and then load it into your face, not choke on a cloud of cheese-scented sawdust. A case can be made for grated Parmesan but really, just get the shaved kind. It's so good and it makes you look Very Fancy. And here's a thing you can do with whatever is left over and you want to pretend that you are craving a salad when actually you just want to eat some cheese:

Mix a few tablespoons of olive oil with the juice of a lemon and some lemon zest, grind some salt and pepper into it, then toss in a few handfuls of watercress or baby spinach. Serve topped with shaved Parmesan. Pat yourself on the back for being so responsible while dousing much-needed nutrients in artery-clogging oil and cheese.

Sometimes I just want a big bowl of something to hug against my chest as I cry into it. Cereal is a no because even if I use almond or coconut milk, fiber is an unpredictable assailant against my digestive system, and I don't want to wake myself up farting. Speaking of, I love a good chili, but as much as I hate Earth I suspect my landlord doesn't actually recycle and all those bean cans going in the real trash fills me with insurmountable guilt. But then again it's not like I'm going to ever soak my own dry beans or can a bushel of San Marzanos (do tomatoes come in a bushel?) and do I feel bad enough about landfills to start? The *real* question is: Why is living so hard? Why am I up at night haunted by that moisturizer jar I realized was made of #7 plastic and can't be recycled after I went to the trouble of rinsing it out? I don't own Walmart! I don't make batteries! Why am I trying to slice my wrist open with the sharpened edge of a non-recyclable frozen low-calorie pizza box when I am just one person with a below-average amount of trash? Anyway, a delicious soup!

A DELICIOUS SOUP

Ingredients

   1 yellow onion, sliced from top to bottom, so you get beautiful half-moon slivers

   2 red peppers, cored and seeded, cut into thick strips

   2 tablespoons butter

   3 teaspoons minced garlic from a jar

   2 teaspoons paprika

   2 tablespoons tomato paste (from a tube; it's easier)

   1 28-ounce can diced tomatoes

   1 can veggie broth

   1 teaspoon sugar

   salt and pepper

   2 teaspoons–ish of dried basil

   heavy cream, to taste

   1 bag garlic croutons, FROM THE STORE, because we are never gonna be the type of people to make our own croutons, are you nuts?!

1. Cut the top and the bottom off the onion, hold it down, then take a paring knife and slice from top to bottom while rotating it on a cutting board. I don't know shit about measurements, because I went to school in America, but try to keep the cuts a quarter inch apart. Or an eighth inch, maybe? I'm not gonna dig around for a ruler, but you get what I'm saying. Thin, but not too thin, crescent moons. Then slice the peppers into thick strips. Cook the onions and peppers in melted butter for 8 to 10 minutes, stirring every once in a while, until they're all slick and shiny.

2. Add the garlic. Now, I haven't minced a clove of garlic since 2003. I don't like peeling that tissue skin off it and inevitably puncturing it with my nail, only to have garlic juice seep directly into my bloodstream through my pores and leave me stinking for the next two weeks, no matter how many times I wash. So I buy the kind in the jar. Without shame. Don't let some asshole trick you into feeling bad about your pre-chopped garlic mush. There's no sous chef on the other side of the kitchen dicing shit up for you. This ain't *Top Chef*.

3. Immediately add the paprika and the tomato paste, and stir for a couple of minutes, then add the tomatoes, broth, sugar, and salt and pepper to taste. Then add a couple shakes or pinches of basil and mix it in, then add a shake or pinch more if you can't see any flecks floating in it. That's how I judge food, by whether it looks like I've done anything. I got this recipe from the Internet, lest I fool you into believing I come from

the kind of people who might pass down culinary traditions, attached to one of those articles that's like "Warm Soups for a Cold, Lonely Night, You Fucking Spinster" or whatever. I love it. It's so easy and it takes maybe twenty minutes start to finish, and when you inevitably slurp down the whole pot over the course of an episode of *Grey's Anatomy* you can console yourself by thinking of all the lycopene and vitamin C (I guess?) you ingested.

4. Bring the soup to a boil and then simmer it for a few minutes on medium heat while you try to remember where you stashed the croutons in the pantry. Locate them, wrestle with the tamper-proof packaging until you give up and rip it open with your teeth, then find your best bowl and wipe the ice cream residue out of it with a damp paper towel. Even though I know it's going to be too fucking hot I can never resist sampling what I'm making and singeing my taste buds while I pretend I can tell whether a hot pot of molten lava requires more cumin. So try not to blister your tongue after you add however much cream you desire and test it to see if it's salty enough.

5. Ladle it into your bowl and then, if you are like me, dump in a handful of croutons and wait a few minutes for them to soften. The soup basically turns them into thick clumps of garlicky sponge, and if you let the croutons bloat up enough you won't even have to chew. You can just sit there intermittently sucking on your McSteamy bread and shouting mean things at Meredith.

forest whitaker's neck

A few months ago I woke up one morning in bed with this dude with whom I was having the most frustrating and confusing non-relationship in the history of ever, and he rolled over and, apropos of nothing, said, "You have the tiniest nipples I have ever seen." Then he rolled over and started texting someone; probably a woman with a normal breast-to-nipple-to-areola ratio. Well, isn't that just exactly what I wanted to hear at eight o'clock on a Monday morning while my chest was still clutched with the panic that I might have leaked leftover vaginal goo onto his crisp white sheets overnight? His tone wasn't necessarily negative, but it wasn't like he was fucking cooing over their minuscule adorableness, either.

It was, for all intents and purposes, a "harmless observation." (Let's pretend for a moment that that is a real thing that can happen.) Okay, a harmless observation made while I was still vulnerable and naked and super self-conscious about maybe having grossly snored for eight-plus hours next to a dude who'd just said he didn't want to be in a relationship with me. *Why, thank you for noticing, kind sir!* Aghast, I glanced down at the crinkly chocolate chips at the bottoms (because they point down; because they graze my ankles; because they get rug burns) of my real-woman tits in horror before snatching the sheet away from him and securing it snugly around my miniaturized shame, turning to face the wall and contemplate whether that observation was evidence of some sort of disappointment on his part. "Yeah, totally weird, right?" I managed feebly, then took back my mental apology for pretending he was someone else while he fucked me from behind.

Has this motherfucker ever met a woman before?! Has no one told him the ladybody rules? Here is what you can say about a woman's body when she has clothes on: "You look great in that!" Or: "Wow, that fits perfectly!" Or: "Damn, I can't wait to undress you!" Or: "No one can tell you bought that on sale!"

And here is what you can say about a woman's body when she has her clothes off: **Absolutely Nothing**. Listen, homie, that thing that you secretly hate about my body? Don't worry—I hate it, too. With every fiber in my weird, fibrous breasts. And I'm the one who has to deal with its daily mockery! Every mark, every scar, every scratch, every flaw: I've seen it, documented it, cried over it, and tried to hide it. Would it kill you to pretend it isn't there? Or that—brace yourself—it might make me mysterious and sexy? That morning a couple of months ago, lying in bed with a dude who frequently insinuated that maybe I wasn't *quite* good enough for him, stark naked and painfully self-conscious about my meat waddle and wrinkly areolas, I decided to write this list.

MY PHYSICAL IMPERFECTIONS:
A SEMI-COMPREHENSIVE LIST BY SAMANTHA IRBY,
A FAT PERSON WITH VISIBLE VARICOSE VEINS

Left Foot
- Inordinately large big toe, peppered with a little sprinkling of coarse hair
- Missing baby toenail
- Mole between second and third toes
- Dark scar on instep from drunken flip-flop accident that resulted in broken foot in 2006
- Remaining toenails could stand to be trimmed

Right Foot
- Large, black circular scar from cutting open my toe while shaving it, *the fucking horror*
- Giant crack on bottom of heel
- Yellow foot bottoms
- Weird raised vein on top

At the end of every sexual relationship, I never cry, because I save my tears for shit like dog food commercials and reality television singing competitions, but I always *want* to because "that dude seemed cool with all my weird moles and dark fleshy patches and holy shit I can never show this wretched body to anyone ever again." It's always that first shower after the breakup when I'm lifting my tits up to rinse the crumbs from underneath that it dawns on me that now I have to go out and find *another* person who won't balk at these flabby arms or whatever.

That is terrifying. Just the thought, right now sitting here at Cara's desk working on this essay, of having to introduce my jelly to a new person who is likely to scrutinize and reject it makes me feel like an asshole. I just don't want to do that anymore. Can't we just lie fully clothed in bed together while holding hands and talking about how good pork belly tacos taste? I don't want to do the "I'm sorry this is my disgusting body" apology jig ever again, nor will there ever be a time that the "just let me keep my shirt on" waltz isn't utterly humiliating. Why must they always argue? Just let me keep this stupid long-sleeved shirt on already.

Left Leg

- Dark brown leather burn from fancy-ass North Face boots three inches above ankle
- Dark red mark from ingrown hair on the upper inside chunk of calf
- Dark pinpoint scar from a mosquito bite I scratched the shit out of this summer
- Short, rust-colored scratch on outside calf
- Giant-circular-pale-bumpy-keloid-scar-thing from a bike accident when I was eight, maybe? The bike flipped over and landed on top of me and holy shit this knee is where I landed
- Several super gnarly-looking purple ingrown-hair scars that serve as reasons one through five (yes, there

are five of them!) why I am never going to shave my
pubic hair down to the wood ever fucking again
- Dark brown inner thigh meat

Right Leg
- Long dog scratch that healed totally ugly
- White dog puncture-wound scar on lower shin
- Raised cluster of purple veins on outer thigh
- Dark scrape on knee
- More dark red ingrown-hair spots (no dick is worth
  this, I promise)
- Gross green veins
- Shit, this leg has some leather burn, too?! Those boots
  are three years old!
- Old bug bite, or zit, or something that kind of looks
  like a herpe

I am covered in what my grandmother called "chocolate
sprinkles" when I was too young to know what "disgusting har-
bingers of cancerous doom" meant—i.e., I am a moley motherfucker. You can dress it up and call them beauty marks if you
want, but they are moles. And I have all the kinds: flat scarlet
ones, teeny raised dots, gnarly brown skin tags that actually get
caught in shit like my zipper. You name the mole, I've got one
somewhere. I have a giant black one in the crease where my right
ass cheek connects to my thigh and I'll just wait over here while
you try to figure out how many dudes have asked, "Is that something I gotta worry about?" while trying to fuck me in the ass.

Here is what the women in my family happen to be blessed
with: giant asses; terrible vision; the worst teeth ever; weird,
patchy, thinning hair right at our rapidly graying hairlines; and

a skin landscape dotted with thousands of moles. My grandma's face looked like a giant chocolate chip cookie. When I was a kid I would sit and stare at them, willing that shit not to happen to me. Now every time I look in the fucking mirror I have nineteen new goddamned spots, and they're always the jagged-edge kind that make me think I have skin cancer but are really just harmless and gross.

Ass and Vag

- That butt mole
- It's pretty much all supersexy large-curd cottage cheese back there
- Scar that I got from an infected bite wound from a goddamned dude. I seriously had to be on antibiotics for two fucking weeks from a human mouth, bro.
- Insanely large mons pubis
- Total baboon pussy: brown outside, neon pink inside
- At this point in the night it is really fragrant down there, whew! And hairy!

Torso

- Waistband skin tag that has nearly been ripped off a dozen times due to comfortable, high-waisted mom jeans
- Big red birthmark on lower belly
- Hyperpigmented waistband shading? Is there a cute way of saying what that is?
- Cinnamon roll
- Treasure trail, which is apparently not sexy if you're a lady

- Streeeeeeeeeeetch marks
- Hyperpigmented underboob from years of underwires holding up these jugs
- Same dude bit me on the goddamned back, left a mark
- I'm, like, seven shades of yellow-brown-black up in here
- Deep, dark shoulder grooves because these tits ain't playing
- There's hair on them!
- My armpits are pretty dark, good thing they're covered in silky tendrils

Arms

- Stretch marks is getting redundant, eh?
- Gigantic, horrid mole that is just, barf
- Right arm has a cluster of red moles that look like flea bites
- Dark elbows covered in chicken skin
- Crescent-moon-shaped birthmark
- Pale, raised scar from when I threw myself down a flight of stairs at age six as protest against accompanying my mother to the grocery store

Neck/Face/Head

- My neck is crazy hyperpigmented; it's basically every shade in the pantone African-American skin collection, from Smokey Robinson to Amistad
- So many moles, goodness
- Teenage-girl acne
- Dry patches

- Oily patches
- Blackhead city around the nose
- I'm still missing that damned tooth
- I need braces, but I'm old, so fuck it
- Itchy, scaly scalp that needs my constant attention
- Sometimes my one eye gets lazy
- Waxy ears, the waxiest
- More moles, seriously
- This dumb hair, which OMG is going gray so fast
- Chin whiskers
- Is that a hint of a mustache?
- Meatbeard

I have dimples, though, two of them! So doesn't that sort of cancel out all this bad stuff? No?! Not even the greenish birthmark on my ass cheek that I missed during the initial analysis of this disgusting pre-corpse? Shit. And those scratchy elbows I left out on purpose?! Fine, then. Fuck it. Love me or don't. High five.

SPENDING THE NIGHT IS THE WORST BECAUSE . . .

Poop

Can I shit in this dude's crib? Like, *really* shit in this dude's actual toilet and shit? I mean, because, um, last night at dinner I ate ten ounces of medium-rare steak and some oozing, cheesy au gratin–y mashed potato thing and I couldn't resist buttering the shit out of that cornbread and I'm pretty sure the grilled asparagus had hollandaise on it and confident women order dessert, right? To prove how progressive we are? Because we don't want to sit there idly poking at a side salad pretending not to be starving half to death?! So I ate that entire molten chocolate flourless salted caramel tower and now it is morning and my stomach is hot/churning/gurgly and I'm pretty sure these walls are so thin that he will hear all the disgusting grunting I'm about to do getting all that sludge out of my body, and I should have just taken a cab and gone the fuck home, why am I so dumb?

Morning

It's just so motherfucking *bright*. Whatever sexiness I feel at 2:00 a.m., shrouded in darkness, cloaked in mystery, is completely erased by the harsh light of the sun. In daylight you can see my little pencil-eraser nipples and that giant red tomato-splotch birthmark on my lower belly. My chin whiskers are out, can he see that shit? How much pore-minimizing, light-reflecting, wrinkle-hiding makeup did I smear on this light-colored pillowcase? Does that long hair belong to me? Did this asshole fuck someone else in the same gritty sheets I just pretended to be asleep in?!

Last Thanksgiving I woke up in the bed of a dude I thought I knew better than I actually did. He didn't have blinds or curtains, and the sun was excruciatingly bright, white-hot and unforgiving. In the middle of the night I had burned my tits on the sizzling radiator trying to sneak to the bathroom because I didn't want to fart next to him in bed and use my asshole as an alarm clock, and I glanced down to see an angry red burn streaked down the side of my boob. Dude woke up and rolled awkwardly on top of me, and I hate banging in the morning, but shit. It was fucking Thanksgiving, for Christ's sake. I was feeling charitable.

Anyway, we're doing it missionary style, in honor of the Pilgrims, and I looked up and saw two alarming things: (1) his eyes were rolling back into his head, which looked so ridiculously insane, and (2) there appeared to be a rather large clump of ladyhair trapped in his beard. And it was dangling precariously close to my face.

Sex in the morning

Dude, I *know* it's a thing. A supposedly hot thing. And if we lived in a movie it would probably be a very sexy thing that I enjoy doing with my perfectly elastic body and my vagina that smells like a new car. But in real life I am so gross at eight o'clock in the morning. And everything in the room is just so *visible*. I start wondering if homeboy has ever heard of a dust rag or a Swiffer cloth. Or how many technical manuals one person can own. Why this motherfucker still has a road atlas. Or if there's anything edible in his fridge. Okay, so I'm underneath this sweaty, grunting dude watching a tangled snarl of some broad's snatched-out weave move closer to my mouth with every thrust. I just kept counting turkeys jumping over a fence (right?) and scooting my head out of the way, thinking that if I had just gone home this wouldn't be happening to me right now. Is it too much to ask a man to take a lint roller to his sheets at the very least? If you aren't going to wash them, is it too much to ask for you to gently shake them out on the back porch?

My toothbrush is not here

And my mouth tastes like a butt. My hair stuff isn't here, either. Why does this dude only have bars of Dial soap? Can I use that shit without my face cracking into a million pieces? Why doesn't he have Vaseline? Or Listerine?! If I could just find a bottle of mouthwash under the sink maybe I could swish with that and use a Q-tip to scrape some of the plaque off my teeth before I have to breathe on him again. That is the worst part of the walk of shame, the tasting of last night's dinner and some dude's dirty balls on my breath while standing awkwardly in line at Starbucks, tongue fiddling with the grime on my teeth. And my hair needs a little water and a little leave-in, otherwise it looks like scattered tumbleweeds atop my head, and all that glancing around the bus trying to assess whether anyone has noticed is downright exhausting. This is the kind of stupid worry that keeps me awake at night. I am an idiot.

Rewearing gross panties with the hardened crotch

You know, because you got superwet while you were making out in the cab on the way home and instead of thinking, "I should probably rinse these soiled underpants in the sink and lay them on a towel on the radiator" when you drunkenly stumbled into his place, your brain was all "Cock fuck bite me right there stick your fingers inside me ouch I can't get my goddamned shoe off kiss me harder does he really sleep on a futon? Bite me again get your dick in my mouth right this minute." Then your panties end up in a pile with all your other shit, slowly turning to stone overnight. That's not just me, right? I know that shit happens to you broads, too. And in the morning when you wake up before he does so you can text your friends, while trying to find the coffee filters in his messy-ass kitchen, to let them know he didn't chop you into a dozen pieces, you remember that you don't have pants on and then holy fucking shit, smelly petrified sexytime panty crotch.

The cat is getting **so fucking mad** *right now*

I didn't know I wasn't going to be coming home, Helen Keller. I didn't know that I should've left three scoops instead of half a scoop to compensate for the crushing guilt that's washing over me because I've neglected your nighttime snack time to instead sit across from this dude who was cuter on the Internet and pretend I didn't want to order the biggest steak on the menu and *all three types* of potato sides (scalloped/mashed/au gratin). I should've cleaned the box, too, but I was already dressed in my patented fifth-date outfit (more cleavage, but with jeans, so it still seems casually unslutty, and maybe some red lipstick) and I didn't want to leave the house smelling like cat ass. So then I come home the next morning smelling like borrowed soap and Old Spice deodorant and your bitch ass is like, "Fuck. You. Look at this nice shirt I shredded in your absence. Feed me and go away again." And I do.

bitches are my jam

PART ONE: BFFS.

Here's why I refuse to worry about Medicare and Social Security, despite the fact that I'll probably need both within the next five years: my end-of-life plan involves settling down in a progressive community with a retired WNBA forward and maybe a small dog who doesn't require a whole lot of exercise or attention. SERIOUSLY. At this point, I'm not going the fuck back to school. As the gap between what I'm into and what "the kids" are into continues to widen, I become less and less convinced that one day I'm going to feel like dragging a desk across a linoleum floor to make a circle with a bunch of nineteen-year-olds so that we might hold hands and discuss the *Iliad*. I already know that I want to spend my old age eating hot wings and sobbing through Lifetime movies, and do I really need a college degree to do that? All my suburban white friends are probably shaking their heads over their plates of wilted arugula and cold beet soup, but I have to be realistic up in here. I work fifty to sixty hours a week, and when I was going to community college in addition to this full-time fucking job, I would get home and literally fall asleep with my head in the algebra book after leaving the class that let out at nine. NINE IN THE EVENING. Then I'd get up and try to figure out integers or some shit while riding the goddamned train to work at seven in the morning. Homeless dudes would be standing over me, rubbing their crusty testicles while correcting my work. "You forgot to carry the one, babygirl." Kill me.

I don't know how you bitches do it. Magazines are always full of some uplifting trifle about a bitch with a crack addiction and nineteen fatherless children who lived in a paper bag while prostituting her way through Princeton, and I'm always stunned. If I get a motherfucking hangnail I'm half an hour late to work and spend the whole day whining about how much it hurts, so I simply CANNOT COMPREHEND how these bootstrap broads pull it together and earn a master's degree while eating one can of soup a week and buying their bras from Walgreens. And I guess that's why my 401(k) will forever have $37 in it, because the minute shit gets difficult and complicated, I quit fucking doing it. I like to sleep a lot and go to Big Star twice a week, and if it takes remaining a goddamned idiot to do that, then that's what I'ma have to do.

HEY, GIRL. Every time I see a Cialis commercial I think, "Oh my fucking GOD, I bet the last thing that old broad wants to do is wait for that old dude to finish raking those leaves while his boner pill kicks in." Isn't the sweet shit about getting old that you don't have to do that shit anymore?! You know she would rather be somewhere with a light pink sweater draped over her shoulders and a pair of magnifying glasses dangling from a chain to nestle in her bosom while watching daytime television, and not rolling down her knee-high beige stockings while waiting for Arthur to turn off Fox News long enough to remove his oxygen mask and bang her for forty-five strong, hard seconds.

Sooner or later every installment of your favorite vagina rag is going to have a section called "Have You Gone Gay Yet?" Or give you a step-by-step guide to transitioning off the penis. These dudes are just doing too much. You know I revel in other people's misery, and I've had SO MANY terrible conversations lately with my ladyfriends who are still climbing back into the dating ring after being TKO'd over and over and over again. Ambiguity, assholery, dickballism, YUCK. And even the positive stories from the fucking frontlines are tempered with "Well, he hasn't been an asshole . . . *yet*." Being on the sidelines is just brutal because, despite this hardened exterior, I'M A SENSITIVE FUCKING PERSON. Listening to some poor girl crying because a dude dumped her over breakfast cereal (true story, men are shit die die DIE) makes me want to cry, too. Women all over the country are sobbing on one another's padded shoulders about all the dumb shit their men are unnecessarily putting them through. And it's inevitable, sooner or later all that commiseration is going to turn into a hand-holding trip to Home Depot. To pick out heated floor tiles.

I hate talking, though. I like e-mailing and texting, and if I could only express my love for a person through smiley and heart emoticons I could die happy. I'm not fucking kidding. And that's why I keep my penis hopes alive, because BITCHES GOTTA TALK.

When I had a roommate I would come home every night and before I could even get my MOTHERFUCKING COAT OFF it was, "How was your day? Are you tired? Did you go anywhere? Did you see anyone? How was work? How is everyone at work? Did you do a lot of work? Were you busy at work? Why didn't you answer when I called you at work? Are you hungry? Do you want pasta? Can I get you some Advil? Do you want a cocktail? What should we watch on TV tonight? Is that what you wore to work? What happened to that red shirt? Did you feed the cats this morning? Is this milk in here spoiled? Did you vacuum last weekend? Why was your toothbrush in the sink when I got home? Do you like this weather? Did you put gas in the car? Did you see that ginger snaps are on sale at Dominick's? Do you want me to get you some when I go there? Why do you still have your shoes on? Aren't you going to take your jacket off? When are you going to put those books away like I asked you to? Why did you leave this laundry in the dining room? Have you taken the recycling out? Samantha Irby, WHY DO YOU STILL HAVE YOUR COAT ON IN THE HOUSE?!"

And I would stand there in the hallway in stone silence, THOROUGHLY DEFEATED, thumbing through my mail that she already "accidentally" opened, getting bludgeoned over the head by questions I had no cognitive ability to answer. Because I worked all goddamned day, bitch, and all I wanted to do was come the fuck home, sit in the goddamned bathtub for twenty minutes, and then EAT THE BIG PIECE OF CHICKEN. I wouldn't speak. I would just go sit in the bathroom while she talked at the back of my head. And before long I'd hear little padded footsteps outside the door. "Well, since you're being so quiet, I'm just going to tell you about my day.

Traffic was terrible, Dunkin' Donuts gave me a CORN muffin instead of a BLUEBERRY muffin and I was SO MAD when I got to work it totally ruined my day, none of the kids did their homework and they all failed the test, the salad I took for lunch was spoiled and I left the low-fat vinaigrette on the counter, my check-engine light came on, and . . . ARE YOU LISTENING TO ME WHILE I AM TALKING TO YOU?"

I'd silently take my bath to the soundtrack of whatever new song she loved on the radio; brush my teeth while listening to how busy Whole Foods was and she only stopped there to get that quinoa salad because SAM LIKES IT and she could make me the same thing for half the money why do you have to be so picky; put on my pajamas while she explained, yet again, why I shouldn't soak the fancy new knives with dish soap and hasn't she already told me that five times and if I'm not going to do it right, why bother doing it at all?! And finally, two hours after walking into the house I paid half the money to rent, my supposed sanctuary, it's so late and my eardrums are so abused that I'm not hungry anymore, I'm not thirsty anymore, all I want to do is get the fuck away from the sound of this asshole's voice. Because I love her to pieces and everything, but if she says one more motherfucking word to me I AM GOING TO CHOKE THE SHIT OUT OF THIS BITCH.

Please tell me how you menfriends tolerate it. Not that any of you deserves a medal, but I can't fathom putting up with all that every day. I lived off and on with women for years, but I at least could shut my door and throw myself across the bed and put my headphones on. I'm convinced she sat at her desk all day, every day, writing a list called "How Sam Is Ruining My Life." She'd get herself all lathered up during the commute home, and the minute she heard my key in the lock every evening she'd step away from whatever dinner she was making me (pro), and light into me about how I left a knife out and hadn't given the plants enough water (MOTHERFUCKING CON). And, by the way, do towels just fold themselves?! Holy fucking shit, GIVE A GUY A BREAK. They lure you in with a home-cooked meal, and as soon as you take your shoes off, BAM. Nag nag bitch bitch nag. We just had a fight a couple of weeks ago during which she sent me TWELVE CONSECUTIVE TEXTS. TWELVE. EACH ONE CONTAINING THE MAXIMUM 160 CHARAC-TERS. And I responded to that onslaught with one word, to which she text-shouted, "IS THAT ALL YOU HAVE TO SAY FOR YOURSELF?!" Sigh.

I don't know if I can do it, man. Maybe I'll have to wait until after I go deaf. AND BLIND.

PART TWO: FRENEMIES

Listen. I've had relationships before. Good ones, bad ones, short ones, long ones, chaste ones, kinky ones, right ones, wrong ones. I've dated tall dudes and short dudes; skinny dudes and fat dudes; old dudes and young dudes; smart dudes and dumb dudes; broke dudes and BALLERS. And never once have I ever, in the history of my vagina's history, rolled over in bed one morning to rest my unfocused eyes on the smelly, dirty, hairy hulk of human flesh lying next to me, farting in my good sheets and digging his uncut toenails into my calf and drooling early-morning gingivitis onto my pillowcase and thought to myself, "You know what, you lucky thing? I bet [enter name of single friend] is TOTALLY FUCKING JEALOUS OF YOU."

GROSS. Jealous is one of those nasty words idiots use to

make themselves feel better about their otherwise mediocre situations, and I hate it. Mostly because, whether or not it is true, JEALOUS is one of those accusations that, once hurled, is very nearly impossible to disprove. Seriously, it sticks. Despite the fact that the allegation is almost ALWAYS untrue and that the unimaginative bitch spewing that lie is a filthy snatchbag of horribleness, it's hard to convince some bystanding third party that you aren't, in fact, JEALOUS AS HELL. It's like if I'm wearing a dress and you're wearing jeans and a T-shirt and I nudge my homie and say, "That bitch is jealous because I'm wearing this dress," and the first thing he thinks is: "YEAH, SHE PROBABLY IS." Never mind that the dress I'm wearing doesn't fit and the girdle I have to wear beneath it cuts into my soft meat and that her jeans look totally normal and fine and great; now that I've planted the jealousy seed it's nearly impossible for the fucking thing not to take root and bloom.

So the tricky little grapevine snuck up on me and informed me a couple of times in the past few days/weeks/months that what I suffer from is an acute case of the jealous. Which is funny because I didn't even know that I was sick! It's just like chlamydia! Don't you hate that? You're walking around all happy and oblivious, having not the faintest idea that some grody disease is festering beneath your skin until someone says, "Hey, girl, you probably should go to the fucking doctor." I mean, I felt a little scratchy in the throat, but I thought that was just some seasonal allergy nonsense. I had no fucking idea I'd been bitten by the jealousy bug. Goddamn it, I don't wash my stupid hands enough. I should probably wear a hat when I go outside and sanitize before rubbing my eyes after touching train rails and whatnot. Is there a cure for this shit? Any broad-spectrum antibiotics I can take?! How do the rest of you lonely, cock-blocking-ass broads keep from coming down with the green flu? Does haterade have antioxidants and shit?!

What's hilarious is that no one has ever accused me of something I might actually be jealous of, like how she can stay awake past 11:00 p.m. on a Tuesday or her ability to expertly use chopsticks. Jealous of your passport full of stamps? MAYBE. Jealous of that dude you hate banging who never picks up his fucking dirty clothes? NEVER. Being jealous because some bitch has a dude is like being jealous of a goddamned stomachache: I've had one before; and while what I did to get it might have been fun, once I'm actually stuck with it, it kind of TOTALLY FUCKING SUCKS. If I knew one single woman who was marrying *up* I might change my tune, but everyone I know is sucking the dick of a regular, broke-ass dude. Show me a girl who relationshipped her way to some prime property, and I might show you my "damn, I'm jealous" face. The first time I heard "Sam's just jealous because I have a man and she doesn't" I almost shit myself laughing. You have a boyfriend, I have a cat. We're even. Helen Keller does everything a dude does: eats my fucking food, does what the fuck she wants, leaves her shit everywhere, ruins all my nice things, and never cleans up after her fucking self. She doesn't tell me what she's thinking, she rarely takes my feelings into account, she doesn't pay attention when I talk, and she only wants affection on her terms. SOUNDS LIKE I HAVE A GODDAMNED BOYFRIEND. Or, at least, it sounds like I have your goddamned boyfriend.

I know a handful of motherfuckers throwing shade at MY ASS while scrolling through their boyfriends' text messages in the middle of the night trying to figure out whether those dudes are seeing someone else. I'm jealous of that, eh? IF YOU SAY SO. (And you totally have been saying so, to more than one of our mutual acquaintances.) You know what I don't have to do? Wonder where my boyfriend is all day. Wonder why my boyfriend didn't answer his cell phone. Wonder why my boyfriend didn't answer his work phone. Wonder why my boyfriend's Facebook is private. Wonder who my boyfriend is texting during dinner. Which totally explains why I'm so jealous and bent out of shape all the time. All of this free time to read books and go to shows and cultivate personal interests can really get to a person.

Is it really so impossible to believe that a single broad can be happy? Is a relationship really the female holy grail?! Would I like to be getting laid? Maybe. Like I've said before, I would much rather get the occasional e-mail from some interested party who would like to fuck me, because actual sex is overrated and uninteresting. (Which I bet you mean girls with boyfriends already know.) All my self-esteem is looking for is some validation. It makes me way happier to continue not waxing my asshole and wearing boring cotton underwear that go from my kneecaps to just below my chin. And, like I've also said before, I've DONE THAT BEFORE. I've had someone who swore he loved me not answer my calls and fuck other girls the minute my back was turned and never pay me back the money he owed me and not keep his promises. I might own up to a little seething envy if I hadn't already done the honeymoon-phase thing. Oh, wait, I get it. Now that it's happening for YOU it's different. Okay then.

And I LOVE love, so I hope that for everyone reading this, that shit *is* different. Unless getting laid on the regular has somehow stricken you with vaginal amnesia and you start saying nasty things about your fucking ladyfriends just because you've got a dick in your box. A pox on you people; for YOU I want nothing more than wilting erections and maxed-out libidos. I was told that someone said, "It's always the jealous friend who messes everything up" in reference to ME, of all people, and on that I call BULLSHIT. Even you happily coupled girls know a bitch or twelve who got a boyfriend or planned a wedding and all of a sudden started treating you like something she scraped off the bottom of her shoe. What is it about being boo'd up that makes some bitches act like they suddenly know some shit? Last week you couldn't tie your shoes without help, bitch, but now that the fear of dying alone has forced you to settle for that dude who works at the gas station, you think you can advise me on what I'm doing wrong in MY life? Yeah fucking right. And I'm an easygoing person, mostly because if I had my druthers I'd never ever have to get out of bed EVER. But I don't hold anyone to strict friendship standards because I don't want them to do that to me, so I climb on in the backseat or slide myself over to the back burner and give her some space to enjoy her mancake. And it isn't hard, because the more time my ladyloves spend with their men, the more goddamned interesting I seem in comparison whenever they finally come up for air.

I love when my homegirls get dudes or my lesbians pair up. Everything in my goddamned apartment was put together (1) by someone else's man, or (2) by a woman with both a vagina and a full beard. I'm not fucking kidding. I can't be changing light bulbs and putting IKEA dressers together! Which is why I need your man and his tool belt to do that shit for me. I throw a goddamned party when my girlfriends get guyfriends, because hanging out with couples means they are probably going to PAY FOR MY DINNER. That $37 they're saving by living together can be used to comp my roast beef, and why the fuck would I ever get mad about THAT? I know that it's easy and comforting to think that I'm sitting alone spraying Helen with Axe and dressing her up in men's suits while drying my tears on a painting of your man I had commissioned, but really I'm thinking of a way to convince you to bring him over so I don't have to get on a ladder and try to change the fluorescent bulbs in my kitchen. Ain't nobody making no voodoo dolls over here. I want you dudes together FOREVER. Because I need someone to take my metal bed frame down to the dumpster.

You know why else I love your man? Because you have to leave the club and go home to him. Which means if I try to slide my number to that Laz Alonso look-alike drinking moscato (gross) at the bar, you can't do anything but go home and tell your MAN about it. Mwahahahaha. And I would accuse you of being jealous of my *Sex and the City* (snort) lifestyle, but then I'd think about how you could turn around and make fun of all the single-serving Healthy Choice meals gathering freezer burn next to the seven half-eaten pints of Ben & Jerry's in my icebox and I would SHUT THE FUCK UP. And let's not act like I have restraint; those ice creams have all the chunks and gooey bits carved out of them. Once all the fudge pieces and peanut butter swirl is gone I have no use for them. Don't act like it's just me.

1. Why I'm not jealous of that dude you're banging

Because he doesn't take you out. You've never seen him in the daytime. You don't TALK about anything. You don't know where he lives. You've never met any of his friends. You haven't seen the inside of his car. I like not having to take STD or pregnancy tests unless I feel like having a laugh. I like not having to figure out "if this is going anywhere" or pretending to be okay with "seeing other people." And I could get anonymously banged if I wanted, and so could any other broad reading this, so let's stop pretending like you're sitting on a magic vagina over there, ladies. Okay? I can supply my own orgasms, and I don't have to shove all my dirty laundry in the closet and hide ten bags of trash in the shower before I consult my vibrator. So get out of here with that noise about how good he is in bed.

Also? I'M PROBABLY BANGING MY OWN DUMB DUDE. The difference, though, is that I understand which dudes you brag about and which ones you don't. Which ones might want to be your boyfriend and which ones won't even commit to a restaurant, let alone a future. Which ones meet your friends and which ones you forget about sometimes because they only call you sporadically. It's so embarrassing when some broad climbs up on that booty-call high horse thinking it's a stallion. WE PEEPED THAT JACKASS, GURL. Now go sit your ass down somewhere and stop thinking you're the only one who got her back blown out this morning.

2. Why I'm not jealous of that dude you're dating

Because everyone you know, and even people you don't know, wants to know "where your relationship is going." You can't have three dinners and a movie date with some dude before the postman, your yoga instructor, the checkout girl at Walgreens, and the bitch who cut your hair that one time three years ago want to know exactly what stage you two have reached. Do you like him? Does he like you? Are you exclusive? Are you sure you're exclusive? Has he taken down his OkCupid profile? Does his ex still call him? When are you moving in together? When are you getting a dog together? Did he give you a set of keys to his car? Are both names on the lease? Is he the marrying type? Has he bought a ring? Is he THINKING about buying a ring? Does he want kids? Does he want kids with you?!

Having a regular sex partner just leads everyone else on the planet to believe that they have a vested interest in your relationship, and I prefer to tell my business to the Internet, thankyouverymuch. I can't think of anything worse than having to fill everyone in on the state of my union all the time. And bitches don't really care; they're just waiting for you to reveal something scandalous or terrible to make themselves feel better. MYSELF INCLUDED. I have not, ever, in the history of ever, repeated a nice story some girl told me about her boyfriend. Because I don't care about surprise flowers at the office. I have, however, told everyone I could think of, including strangers on the street, about the dude who took a dump in your hair, or the other one who got your sister pregnant. Because I am a big fan of cautionary tales. And the opposite of jealous.

3. Why I'm not jealous of that dude you're marrying

Because I know a lot of divorced bitches. And a lot of broke-ass couples. Listen, I can be regular by myself. I would like to get married for better health insurance. Or regular access to a decent car.

I need someone I could roll over and borrow fifty dollars from who understands that when I say "borrow" I mean "I'm never giving this back to you." Every time a bitch on a budget turns her nose up about my not having someone to file my taxes jointly with I just think, "Well, what did yours come with?" Bad credit? A mountain of debt that you're now half responsible for? None for me, thanks. And I would rather be dead than tell some dude my ATM PIN, let alone give him carte blanche with my money. I'm thrilled to pieces that you have to sit down at the kitchen table once a week with a shoe box of receipts and explain to a grown fucking man why having money to pay the electric bill is more important than upgrading his game console, but please wake me up when we get to that part that makes me feel bad about myself. Maybe the noise from that bouncing check will be loud enough to do it.

I've never in my life said that I want to be married. Which is why I was left scratching my noggin at the assertion I might not be anything but happy for someone who is. I have very specifically said that I'd like someone to count my pills and make sure I end up in the best nursing home, but that does NOT have to be a husband. As a matter of fact, it's more likely that my care will actually be up to my standards if it isn't. I like my name. I like being able to tell a dude to kick rocks without having to take him to court to do so. "Till death do us part" is a BIG COMMITMENT, man. And I'm not ready for that. Am I impressed and happy that some of you are? YES. Am I dying inside because I haven't yet had the opportunity to plan an overblown party I'm too broke to pay for? ABSOLUTELY NOT. I'm not ready to sign up for having some dude be my problem for THE REST OF MY LIFE.

If I wanted someone to nag and yell at all the time I'd have a goddamned baby. And besides, most weddings are just a parade of everything you couldn't really afford to do, and I'd much rather stress myself out trying to save up the money to spend my summer on a boat in the Bahamas instead of catered crab puffs and shrimp toast.

So for all you gorgeous girls braiding your armpit hair and leaving shit in the toilet for a day and masturbating while you stand at the kitchen sink, this is for you. Keep enjoying your alone time and only having to look after your own socks. And make sure you put a NuvaRing on it.

PART THREE: LOVERGIRLS.

Women know how to make shit comfortable. If I never got banged on a king-size bed with NO SHEETS and ONE LUMPY PILLOW ever again in my fucking life it would be too goddamned soon. Dudes always want to try to fuck you in the abandoned warehouse in which they're squatting. Or at least that's what the shit fucking looks like, all bare walls and "furniture" procured from alleys and shit. Would it kill you motherfuckers to put a mat in the bathroom? To buy soap with a moisturizing agent? To have anything other than Gatorade or Muscle Milk or power juice in your fucking refrigerator? To put all twenty-seven pairs of Jordans in a closet rather than the arranged display over which I am *bound* to stumble in the middle of the goddamned night?! I like soft things that smell awesome. I like multicolored Le Creuset rubber spatulas. I like coffee mugs with handles. I like fresh gerbera daisies. Which is why I have to learn to like strap-ons. Or marry a gay man.

Why do you dudes only own one towel? And a hand towel at that?! Why do you have no paper towels? Why is all your shit in garbage bags even though you moved in two years ago? Why does it smell like gym shoes and testicles in your apartment? Why do you refuse to purchase a fitted sheet at the very least? Do I really have to SLEEP IN MY GODDAMNED CLOTHES TO STAY WARM UP IN HERE? Why don't you have blankets? Why do you need so many remotes? Why do you have a roommate at forty-two? Why do you own a leather couch and a 573-inch flat-screen but not a single motherfucking plate? Do we really have to share cutlery?!

Every time I have nearly broken my goddamned neck tripping over the twenty-plus Wii and PlayStation and Xbox cords in the dark in some dude's raggedy house trying to find my way to the bathroom that has paper towels in lieu of toilet paper and a cracked and dried-out bar of Dial melted into the sink I think, "I really have to start fucking women." And eventually won't we all? Standing in the cold and dark, feeling beard stubble and dirt from outside being ground into your bare feet (why did you get that predate pedicure again?), shaking your hands dry because you used the last square of one-ply toilet paper to try to soak up whatever droplets of postsex pee it could absorb, you mean to tell me you didn't wish HE was a SHE? Or that you were at least in your own fucking house? Where there is plenty of toilet paper?!

You won't want to eat at my house because Crohn's food is awful (dry toast!) but you'll want to do every goddamned thing else. There are nice candles everywhere and dozens of expensive soaps and lots of blankets and clean, crisp sheets. There are paper towels and toilet paper and hand towels and bath towels and a rug and both a shower curtain AND a liner in the bathroom. And dudes don't have the market cornered on technological fun shit. I have a little flat-screen! A couple hundred DVDs! Ten thousand records! A Mac! An Evo! Three iPods! THE INTER-NETS! If I bought a fucking video game system you'd never have to goddamned leave. Especially since Peapod is the jam. I'm not saying a dude has to have an interior decorator, because that is moist, but 99 percent of them can't even clear the empty McDonald's and Taco Bell bags from the bed before trying to put it in your butt. Come on, man! You're getting special sauce in my pussyhole! And NOT the sexy kind.

I refuse to plot and hunt and trap a man only to spend the rest of my life trying to get him to turn off ESPN and pick up a book that doesn't have pictures in it, let alone being the only one in the house who cares enough to buy paperwhite bulbs in season and change the plug-in when it starts to get all dried out and ineffective. I mentally and emotionally cannot cope with being the one who notices that the curtains need to go to the cleaners and the knives in the drawer are all dull. That is exhausting and robs you of your joy. So I'm just going to be a dude and be happy all the time. Just not in the ways that suck. I am going to make a bitch feel so amazing that she'll be falling all over herself to let me lounge on the plush couch in her comfortable house that smells like pinecones or pumpkin pie or whatever scent Martha Stewart says is hot this year. And I will NOTICE that pinecone scent! I don't give a shit about staying in and having a romantic evening for two; I am going to order shit on pay-per-view in my jammies while she takes recipes she printed off of Rachael Ray's website and tries them out in the kitchen, getting drunk on white wine and listening to the Indigo Girls. Sounds like a perfect night to this asshole, especially if she keeps refreshing my plate of chewy cherry chicken cheesies. Or naughty nachos on noodles. Or bacon brisket brownies. Or crazy carrots and crackers. Or eatza meatza pizza. (You get the idea. Rachael Ray is blarf.)

I like laying around without a bra on in cozy, shapeless inside clothes and passing out drunk on boxed wine at 9:00 p.m. in front of a Lifetime movie, and those things make me an ideal lesbian. Plus, I don't have to be reminded to change the cat box and I know how to properly make a bed with a duvet. In other words: I'm perfect.

I could eat a bitch out, I guess. The first thing Laura and Ginger asked me, simultaneously, when I said my sapphic ass was steering my canoe toward the island of lesbos was "But would you GO DOWN ON A WOMAN?" My answer? "TOTALLY." I like oysters and mussels, so what's the problem? I'll just pretend it's a taco and sprinkle a little lime juice and chili oil on it. Nom nom nom. Seriously, how hard could it be to have sex with a goddamned lady? I have TWO EARS and the same goddamned anatomy, so what's the big deal? "Hey, girl, what kind of sexing do you like?" I'll ask, and when she answers, I will LISTEN TO HER and then DO WHAT SHE SAYS. What a novel idea, right? You dudes oughta take note. Fucking really is that easy.

HAVE YOU EVER HAD SEX WITH A MAN? If he's not pounding away, oblivious, at every orifice on your body like you're a fucking blow-up doll, he's outrageously overselling his abilities only to mimic some dumb shit he saw on RedTube once he gets his dick out in your presence. And then he'll have zero qualms about leaving you 100 PERCENT UNSATIS-FIED. And *that* is only if he can maintain a fucking erection. Do you know how many times I have had to say, "My vagina is not your hand, asshole" to some Neanderthal dude who was rabbit-fucking so rough my sensitive meat was chafing and shooting sparks? GODDAMN YOU. And why are you trying to force the head of your penis through the back of my skull? PLEASE STOP FUCKING MY FACE SO HARD, SIR. Even the "sen-sitive" dudes! Once you get them naked they just do whatever the fuck they want, no matter what you said will get you off or what you told them works best for you. They really just do whatever the hell works for them, and if you happen to have an orgasm, too, that's just icing on the cake. Pfffft. Just reading this makes me never want to have sex with another dude for as long as I live, and I'm sure there's some old softball coach who installed her own heated bathroom tiles out there who feels the exact same way.

And goddamn it, I have fucked every single CUNNILIN-GUS EXPERT and ORGASM SPECIALIST in the fucking city of Chicago. Apropos of nothing, dudes always want to tell you how amazing they are at banging. Always. You could ask what type of food this motherfucker eats and he'll be all, "Baby, you know what I really love to eat? Pussy." EXAGGERATED EYE ROLL. "Great, blind date whom I've never met before and am not sure I'm even going to fuck, but where should I make our DINNER RESERVATION?" Bla-arf. It's infuriat-ing. Every dude I've ever met claims to have a PhD in fucking, and that proclamation is usually made before we've even fin-ished the first (inter)course at a restaurant he can't really afford. I can barely get my water refilled before dude is trying to tell me how he makes bitches squirt and shit. And that is lame. I wouldn't care about a little harmless braggadocio after he's slayed this dragon in bed, but before we've even established that his fire hose can temper the flame? YEAH fucking RIGHT.

I don't have to tell some hot lady I'm the president of pussy-town or whatever; I just have to show up with my suitcase of sex goodies and ask which hole she likes the vibrator in. Women use ChapStick and floss their teeth and file their toenails; we spray perfume behind our knees and replace our fancy underpants frequently; we make bruschetta for fun and buy good wine and fold cashmere throws over the arm of the couch in case our company gets cold during movie night. Now, who couldn't cozy up with a little bit of that? Most grown women know how and where they like to be touched, and if a dude ever bothered to pay attention I wouldn't be writing this. A little "Where is your

G-spot?" can save everyone involved a whole lot of goddamned trouble. Basically, I'm going to do the opposite of everything men do. Because they do just about everything wrong. Guaranteed success.

Making a woman happy is easy. You know what makes me happy? Unexpected phone calls in the middle of the day. Remembering what I liked at that one restaurant we went to that one time. Half-dead grocery store flowers just because they were on sale. A good-morning text that reads, "Have a good day and try not to burn anything to the ground in a furious rage." I think dudes like to pretend that we're so difficult both to please and comprehend, but that's got to be because they watch too much dumb shit on television. Sure, there are broads who aren't happy unless a man is subjugating himself at her feet while direct depositing his paychecks into her account, but for the most part she is the exception. The rest of us are just trying to get a phone call every few days and maybe get banged twice or three times a month.

And that I can totally do. Burn up a few anytime minutes and tinker around in her tool shed every once in a while? Totally. I'll even buy a twenty-dollar bottle of wine and rent *Chocolat* on DVD. I will prepare a beautiful dinner, keeping in mind that she hates both onions and smelly cheeses, and serve it on one of my many PLATES, accompanied by an actual GLASS. She won't have to pout alone in the bedroom because my boy Tee and I decided to order the fight on pay-per-view, nor will she have to worry that *I'm* the one who got her friend Judy pregnant. I won't ever ask to "hold a few dollars" or borrow her car to go drop some formula money off at my baby mama house. Fuck all that. I'm going to go roll my eyes through her book club meet-

ings, listen to her Josh Groban CDs in the car without com-
plaint, continue building my shrine to our patron saint, Rachel
Maddow, wear pink-ribbon T-shirts and cargo shorts, obsess
over the kitten colony I started in her basement, and let her go
down on me every night while I watch *Conan*. In other words,
come age forty-five? My shit is about to get awesome.

a bearded gentleman

My perfect man is a woman named Angie Frank. She plays rugby and bikes for charity. She is just the right amount of adorable, like if you mixed a pug puppy with a nine-year-old boy. She's basically the nicest person you've ever met. And it's not what she is, it's what she does. She gets up early and makes her partner a smoothie before she even wakes up. She walks their dogs during snowstorms. She runs and gets the car so we don't have to stand outside in the rain or walk four blocks to where she parked teetering in our fancy shoes. Basically, she's perfect. But that bitch already has a lady, and those jerks seem happy together, so until I can figure out how to poison a hoe without anyone suspecting me, here's what I want from my most-perfect person:

I. MASCULINE. Where are the motherfuckers who smell like whiskey and gasoline? Where are the motherfuckers who climb up on the roof to fix shit? I don't want to fuck a dude who has a "hairstyle." I want a grizzly bear with a near-constant erection to boss me around and pay for shit while LOOKING LIKE A MOTHERFUCKING MAN. Or a manly lady. I'm into that.

2. BOOKS. Not a sports page, not a magazine, A FUCKING BOOK. Or takes a class. Anything that makes his brain work.

3. PASSPORT. This isn't really as much about seeing the world as it is about only having sex with A GROWN-ASS GOD-DAMNED MAN. Everything on this list pretty much boils down to "let's stop banging manchildren." Seriously, you only speak one language and you don't have a bank account and you have to go "put minutes on your phone" and I'm supposed to let you fuck me in the ass on the third date?! Yeah, right. We aren't doing that anymore. I'm tired of dicking around with stunted adolescents. There can only be one of those in my life, and that is me, homie. You need to go to the doctor regularly and shit.

4. PATIENT. Celibate for seven months and the shit feels amazing. I may never go back! I'm doing this new thing where I try to wait more than half an hour to bang a dude I'm into because I read all those articles about oxytocin and I'm terrified of becoming chemically bound to some asshole who just wants to fuck my hot friends. I AM NOT SMARTER THAN BIOLOGY. I don't think a handful of interactions is an unreasonable expectation before I subject my neurotransmitters to a bunch of powerful hormones that are going to make me weak-kneed and starry-eyed over a guy who is going to give me the "just friends" speech next week. And he should be cool with that, however long it takes.

5. NICE. I don't mean "won't punch you in the face." That shit is a given. I'm talking basic consideration: doesn't play mind games; doesn't talk shit about my body; doesn't lie to me all the goddamned time. Nice too often gets a bad fucking rap. You hear "nice" you think "weak," so you go find someone dangerous and exciting, which are really just euphemisms for MEAN. God, I just don't want to suck anymore thoughtless dicks, you know? Look, sir, I'm not saying you have to turn my apartment into a greenhouse or whatever, but if you could send some flowers a couple of times a month as a thank-you for that repulsive thing I allow you to do inside my delicate meathole it would make me feel like a goddamned champion. Remembers my motherfucking birthday, offers to stop by with some broth when I am dying and choking up lungbutter, keeps a few cans of ginger ale for me in his fridge: THIS IS MY DATING FUTURE.

6. BEARDED. MEATY.

would dying alone really be so terrible?

I tell anyone who is interested that my ideal long-term romantic relationship is one in which my manfriend and I have separate apartments in the same building. Or in buildings across the street from each other. Or buildings on opposite sides of town. Or opposite sides of the state. I have very little interest in joint cohabitation. Seriously, almost none, save for the fact that if a dude had a big TV and was willing to pay for premium cable and give me seventy-thirty ownership of the remote, THEN I would maybe consider it. I mean, come on. His and Hers houses?! TOTAL JAM.

I don't know, man. I'm just not big on spending every waking minute with someone you show your privates to. People are boring. I'm fucking boring. My funny runs out; my cute runs out; my smart sometimes hiccups; my sexy wakes up with uncontrollable diarrhea. I have a fucking attitude. And a sharp, nasty edge. I'm impatient. I like the whole fucking bed. I hate anyone touching and moving my artfully disheveled possessions all the time. I'm a downright terrible sharer, and I can't guarantee that I won't write my name on something in the refrigerator I don't want you to eat.

I have neither the time nor patience to fix thirty-plus years of all my gross shit. My snoring, my shitting all the time, my only flushing the toilet after I've peed in it a bunch of times, my irregular mopping, my gross litter box, my dinner in bed, my counter covered with pill bottles, my cat food everywhere, my cat hair everywhere, my piles of filthy laundry, my dozens of dirty-ass Birkenstocks scattered all over. Sometimes Helen gets maxi pads out of the bathroom trash and chews them. Sometimes I let food go bad and take way too long to throw it out. Sometimes I drink out of the same water glass for, like, three days without washing it. BARF.

I want to still have time to sit staring at the wall for hours with both my headphones and the television on, zoning. I want to watch porn by myself, because a dude just won't let you take five minutes to masturbate without his dick thinking it's an invitation, and then that five minutes becomes twenty-five minutes (if you're lucky) of heat and sweat and effed-up hair and having to remake the bed and being late for work and even then, after all that grunting and shoving and groaning, you might STILL have to get your vibrator out while this motherfucker passes out on top of the shirt you'd taken out to wear to the office.

I stand in my kitchen with an open container of Nutella and an open container of honey-roasted Skippy peanut butter, and I dip a butter knife first in one and then the other, then I try to lick it off in such a way that each glob is a fifty-fifty mixture of each. I can't do that horrifying shit if I live with some foxy dude. I mean really, do you think he's going to lie there looking all hot and awesome and still want to rip me out of my chonies after watching that? The answer is no. No, he will not. But I still want to do it. So that means no living together. Because I can keep my apartment clean and safe and inviting for a night, for a weekend, for maybe even a week, but that day-to-day shit ain't happening. I am obviously going to die alone, in giant panties that come up to my chin, with crumbs under my tits, and a half-eaten cat face.

i really don't eat this much salad!

Congratulations on dumping me! I know what a harrowing decision it must have been after four insanely fun months of sticking your dick in awesome, and I'm heartbroken that you had to make it all by yourself. But what a motherfucking relief, right? To be rid of this stupid albatross? You could've called me! I would've helped you! We could have gone over the pros and cons together, as a team, like friends! Because that's what friends are for! You know how you're always saying that we're friends? Like, when I accidentally left my toothbrush on the sink and you politely reminded me that friends take their belongings with them as you handed it to me when you dropped me off at the train early that one morning? So I'm surprised that you wouldn't at least text me, your buddy your pal your friend, for support and advice when making this monumental decision.

·····

OH MAN, right now I am living in a post-breakup body. A totally destroyed meaty pre-corpse, hairy and dirty and kind of smelly despite my Earth-friendly deodorant. And it's fall, so no one is going to give me a hard time for wearing a hoodie and dark jeans every single day of the week, which is why that's what I have worn every single day of this week. Yesterday I wore pajamas as real clothes to brunch, and sunglasses as big as my face, which I also tried to hide with one of those big scarves that are so fashionable these days. I haven't had a shower in three days because I'm too goddamned tired to take a motherfucking shower. Is that even a thing? I left the house this morning and took my laptop to Pillars so I could stare out at real people actually enjoying their productive lives while pretending to work. This blond twentysomething has walked her fluffy Pomeranian past this coffee shop half a dozen times. I'm not even kidding. She's wearing pink sweatpants that probably have "I like anal" emblazoned in glitter across the backside, and that dog looks like a real pain in the goddamned ass.

When we were together and he was over all the time, I actually went grocery shopping. And it's sad, or it's something worse than sad, that I hauled big bottles of Voss up three flights of stairs once a week so that he would be impressed by my fancy choices. I hid Filet-O-Fish wrappers at the bottom of the garbage, so he wouldn't know that I didn't eat roasted brussels sprouts and wild-caught salmon every night. I am a person who squeezes Easy Cheese onto a slice of bologna and rolls it up like a carcinogen burrito at least twice a week. But dude was always appraising my cabinets, turning his nose up at my salty snack foods, and asking why the bananas weren't organic. "BECAUSE THE CORNER STORE DOESN'T SELL ORGANIC FRUITS, MUTHAFUCKA" is what I wanted to shout on my tiptoes right up in his face but instead I let him shame me. And the next time I got organic bananas.

It's too bad you didn't reach out, because I could've helped you avoid looking like such a fucking prick. I would have advised against the Facebook message to end things. I mean, come on, dude. Are we fourteen? That's really how little you think of me? Update your status, skim through a few Huffington Post *links so you can pretend to be a well-informed member of the electorate, make a few moves in* Words with Friends, *share three of those dumb inspirational infographics, and send me half a paragraph about how sorry you are that things weren't going to work out the way you'd hoped? Nice way to start a Tuesday. I mean, I wasn't even getting attached until you made me feel like it was okay to get attached. And now I've been punished for something I hadn't even wanted to do in the first place.*

I am not going to reactivate my dating profiles. Not for a while. Not for a really long time. Maybe not ever. I am officially too jaded for this shit. This song and dance, where he's singing one song and I'm dancing to another and by the time I realize that we are moving in opposing rhythms it's already too late. I'm not a dumb asshole anymore. I don't make bad decisions or fuck bad people anymore, not like I did when I was a kid, yet I'm always left blindsided and dumbfounded at the end of a thing, the end of a thing that I thought was one thing and was surprised to find out was totally another. It's so hard, because we are all just these vulnerable little babies who are trying to stick and move before we're caught with our guards down. If doing that felt good I would keep doing it. If it was worth it, I would keep doing it. But my love life makes me feel like a feral cat backed into a corner: spine arched, hackles raised, teeth bared, snarling and hissing at any potential liars or cheaters or opportunists who dare to get too close. I hate this idea that women are just bitter of our own accord, that we haven't been driven there by years of taking it on the chin while trying to maintain a cheerful disposition.

Bitter. Scariest word in the entire dictionary. Meanest word there ever was. Nastiest tasting word to have in your mouth. I would almost rather be called a cunt, right to my fucking face, than to have some dismissive asshole refer to me as bitter. I'm not bitter; I survived a liar. I'm not bitter; I weathered a cheater. I'm not bitter; I sustained a massive injury to the giant, bloody muscle in the center of my chest that is responsible for pumping blood through my entire body. So this hostility you've encountered isn't the result of my ingesting too many sugar-coated romantic comedies and metabolizing them into virulent hatred for real-life men with all their salt and their human mistakes. That would be amazing, if I could just skip weathering all this heartbreak to instead compare and contrast every prospective boyfriend against the character Denzel played in that one movie I liked. But no, I came by these feelings honestly. And I don't accept bitter. Wounded, yes. Traumatized, sure. Grieving, okay. Anything other than bitter. I put too much work in to be callously tossed aside as bitter. Bitter is for someone who hasn't earned it.

· · · · ·

I don't really eat this much salad! I don't go to the gym as often as you think I do! My legs are never this smooth! I only trim my toenails in case you happen to look down at them! I happen to enjoy my armpit hair! Manicures hurt my fingers and I always fuck them up and I hate spending money on something I can do myself but I only did it because you noticed! No, your jokes are not funny! I hate nature programs! I only have a subscription to The Economist *to look smart! I love watching bad TV, like really, really love watching bad TV. I like pork loin! The newspaper bores me! I am not smart enough to finish the crossword after Wednesday! I only want to wear flip-flops! I like John Grisham novels! I hate being outside! Celebrity gossip is better than regular news! Sometimes I don't shower for two days in a row! I never change my sheets this often! Bleaching the bathroom every other minute is exhausting! I hate waxing my pubes! Fancy underwear is for assholes! Lingerie is for douchebags!*

After the third date I go out and buy some new things. A few pairs of sheer and frilly underpants, a couple of new hot bras. I'm not a total asshole; I like to be excited about things. And that's when the relationship is the best: when there have been a couple of good dinners and a handful of the kinds of texts that make you smile in the middle of an otherwise dreary workday, and instead of dreading what is sure to be some awkward and uncomfortable first new sex, I am thumbing through a table full of black lace, brimming with hope and eager with anticipation. I've done the jokes and the sparkling conversation, and now I am doing all the tedious shit that I am supposed to do to get myself sexready. Because this person, to whom I have issued a clean slate and given every benefit of the doubt, deserves my best effort. Until it isn't enough for him, because so far I've never been enough for any him, and I no longer have to keep up the ruse that I enjoy baking my own bread or listening to classical music podcasts. But I also don't have to parse through a bunch of word salad to figure out whether I'm being lied to. I don't have to count the number of hours I haven't heard from him, or wonder if I'm texting too much, or panic that sending that third e-mail was a terrible idea, or try to decipher the hidden meaning in the voice mail he just left. I can finally fucking relax again, with my dirty humidifier and my fat-free pudding for dinner without being under some dude's microscope. This wasn't a relationship, this was a girlfriend pageant, and I made first runner-up. So I am taking off my sash and scrubbing off this lipstick. I prefer to think of it as "keeping it disgustingly real" rather than "letting myself go." Because I feel like if I'm still bothering to wash my hair and take a multivitamin once in a while and read an old issue of *Newsweek* at the doctor's office then I haven't let go, I've just loosened my grip.

thumbsucker

What do you pack for a grown-up pajama party? What stuff do you need in order to make sure your walk of shame is as minimally humiliating as possible? Often to my detriment, I am one of these people who is concerned with appearing *needless* and *aloof* when mired in some sort of bullshit romantic relationship that, when it comes to the "why don't you just spend the night at my place after dinner?" suggestion, makes the possibility of a casual sleepover an exercise in batshit crazy ladybrain overload. I never want to be so presumptuous that I potentially scare the shit out of someone I've only known for a handful of weeks who isn't really convinced whether he'd really like to be in a relationship with me. But I also don't want to spend the next day at work smelling like Old Spice deodorant with dry cheeks and dusty hair.

So then I'm home, sweating while tiptoeing around my apartment in my bra and Spanx, getting ready for this dinner that is merely a formality prior to "WHY DON'T YOU JUST SLEEP AT MY PLACE TONIGHT?," trying not to fuck up my drying nails despite the sudden urge to play guitar/wash the dishes/repot all the plants, and I'm faced with the harrowing decision of what to pack in the overnight bag: Should I assume he has decent soap? Do I really need a night cream and a toner? How many pairs of panties do I need? Will he have a spare toothbrush I can borrow, or should I bring my own? Why did I buy all these gallon-size bottles of styling cream? This is what I usually bring: one pair of reasonably adorable yet nonslutty underwear, a toothbrush because I can't deal with plaque teeth for even a minute, and a stick of deodorant, because I stink a lot and sometimes showering in a dude's dirty sweatsock bathroom is more trouble than it's fucking worth. I don't want to get testicle fungus on the bottoms of my goddamned feet, bro. Also, especially if you buy airplane travel sizes of shit, you can fit all that stuff in an oversize clutch and not look like you're moving in after the third date. Fourth, if you're a prude.

So I pack the rest of my unassuming womanbag (Kindle in case he's boring, cab fare in case he's crazy, Imodium because I am not ready to shit at his house yet), and get on my date clothes and check my lipstick and spritz the ass of my pants with some Jo Malone and guiltily overfeed the cat when the dread of realization washes over me: I am not sleeping at home this evening. Would it be weird if I brought my blanket? AND WHAT THE FUCK AM I GOING TO SAY ABOUT MY GODDAMNED THUMB?

I have a really embarrassing secret to tell you, but you have to promise me that you won't ever tell anyone else. Pinkie swear?

Okay, here goes: I am a grown-up and I still suck my stupid fucking thumb. Oh, I know, it's hard to believe that the confident, stunningly attractive goddess you've come to know and love could be plagued by such a filthy habit, but the shit's true. There has never been a time that I haven't sucked my thumb. At least not that I can remember. The majority of my early childhood photos involve me smiling around the finger in my mouth. And I'm not sure at what age you're supposed to stop. But I never could. Still. Almost thirty-three years old and every time I get in bed I do so with my built-in pacifier.

Also, I have this blanket. I bought it six or seven years ago, WITHOUT SHAME, from the newborn section at Target. It was sea-foam green when I purchased it, but now it's a sort of dishwater gray. It's from the Carter's Just One You collection, I think? All identifying information has mostly been rubbed off. It's a smooth cotton on one side, with an inch-wide satin border, and the entire back is silky pale green satin. When I was young I had a giant maroon blankie. It had a thick satin edge that I would fold and rub at night to calm down and soothe myself to sleep. I had that disgusting fucking thing until I was nineteen years old. What had once been a queen-size blanket was whittled down to a scrap no bigger than a medium T-shirt by the time I reached middle school. I dragged that nasty thing around like Linus, and my mom would cut it into smaller and smaller pieces, trying to preserve as much of the satin edge as she could. By high school it was the size of a handkerchief. It was totally fucking gross and I was embarrassed to have it, but not so much that I would ever dream of parting with that grimy, disease-ridden rag. Washing it was out of the fucking question. I hid it under my pillow during the day and made a beeline for it the minute I got home. Thumb, blanket, daydreams about boys

I was in love with—life was good. I took that dirty scrap with me to college, sheepishly explaining to my dear sweet roommate Cara that I was basically an emotional mess who relied on this tiny piece of filth to function somewhat normally, and the summer after that first year, one of the dogs I was house-sitting chewed up what was left of my most prized possession. I thought, "Maybe this is a sign. I'm going to quit once and for all." But I couldn't.

It's the left thumb that is my cruel mistress. Tempting me even now as I type this. Upon close inspection you can see that it is flatter than my right, the padded side covered in these faint little cracks that have developed after thirty fucking years of being wet all the goddamned time. I'm right-handed, see, so it was only natural that while I was coloring or twisting a lock of hair between my fingers or rubbing the satin edge of a baby blanket raw with my dominant hand that my left would find its place firmly between the teeth that I have pushed right out of my fucking face to accommodate it. I shudder to think of all the toxic nail polish I've ingested. Of all the flu germs I've swallowed. My throat is like a fucking petri dish in a horror movie.

I suck my thumb when I'm tired. You can always tell when I'm sleepy. The pupil of my right eye starts to slide lazily toward the outer corner; I blink once every ten seconds, my breath lengthens, and inevitably, when I think you aren't paying close attention, I slip my plug in. Forefinger resting gently on my left temple, the other three fingers curled in front of my nose. It's downright adorable. Until you remember that I have a retirement plan.

I suck my thumb when I'm happy. Because you can't always throw a fucking parade when something goes your way. And bragging is rude.

I suck my thumb when I'm sad. Now, let's be perfectly clear: I would much prefer to eat my feelings. OH GOD, the glorious concoctions my depression would come up with if I let it wild out on its own. Broccoli cheese brownie squares, chocolate pudding mashed potato corn nachos, caramel cookie dough pizza bites: I WOULD EAT ALL THE DIABETES. Unfortunately those aren't real things. And making them when I am feeling lonely and neglected would take too much effort and cause a great deal of embarrassment at the grocery store. So, when I'm fresh out of Ben & Jerry's Bacon Truffle Red Velvet Hot Dog, my thumb does the trick. It's better than fucking Prozac.

I suck my thumb while writing. And while watching TV. And while reading books. Pretty much any relaxed, comfortable thing that I can enjoy in relative privacy is accompanied by the preferred coping mechanism of toddlers everywhere. I just sit at my desk with my blanket over my shoulder (or sometimes wrapped around my head) and stare at the screen until the words come. Or until I decide that I'm just going to lie down for a minute and let the ideas come that way. Yeah, right.

I suck my thumb when I masturbate. I know, dude. There is some deep mental illness at work here; I fucking know. Some Freudian pseudo-sexual psychological bullshit I am not smart enough to comprehend, I'm sure. I wasn't breast-fed enough. Or I was breast-fed too much. Saw too many dicks at a young age or some other weird fucking shit. I can't explain it, but it just feels good. Thumbelina, a set of nipple clamps, and a vibrator are pretty much all I need once I win the lottery and can afford to buy an island where I can walk around with my thumb in my mouth all day and not worry about what a crazy person that makes me.

And when I'm getting banged. Only from behind, though,

because anything else would really be totally fucking weird. Could you even imagine that shit?! Anyway, most of the time these assholes don't even notice. And if one does and says something awkward I just deflect and respond with something disgusting or offer to let him stick his thumb in there and usually that's enough to forget the strange interaction we just had.

My parents tried three increasingly ridiculous methods to try to curb my thumbsucking.

1. **NIGHT SOCKS.** This one is simple: a pair of men's athletic socks, one firmly placed on each paw before bed. The first night, I took them off while asleep. The morning after the second night, my mother walked in to find me sucking my socked thumb. Sucking. My thumb. Through. The motherfucking. Sock. Time for a bigger gun.

2. **BITTER NAIL POLISH.** I was not generally allowed to wear nail polish. Wait, let's amend that: I was allowed to wear nail polish on my pinkies only. So when my mom suggested that a manicure might cure me I was pretty fucking excited. Little did I know that she was just going to paint some bitter shit that tasted like butts on my thumb and sit back and watch me foam at the mouth like a rabid dog every time I subconsciously stuck it in my piehole. After a few nights I got used to the taste and the drooling started to level off. Into the garbage went the bitter topcoat.

3. **A HORRIFIC METAL CONTRAPTION THAT WAS AFFIXED TO THE ROOF OF MY MOUTH.** It looked like a fucking fry basket. The dentist hooked it to my

upper molars, this sturdy metal scoop with thin bars
that curved from the back of my mouth to where it fit
snugly behind my front teeth. You couldn't see it from
the front, but the idea was that this cage prevented my
thumb from resting comfortably in my mouth and that
would deter me from sucking my thumb. My mom was
so excited, sure that we were really about to solve this
humiliating problem. What the dentist didn't say was
that half of every solid meal I ever ate would wind up
trapped in the sink catch lodged in my motherfucking
mouth. I'm one of those "foods shouldn't touch unless
they need to" people, and nothing was more horrific
than having salad and meat and bread all mixed together
and trapped precariously close to my tongue. I would
take toothpicks and scrape out the better part of my
dinner, then rinse with a Waterpik to try to dislodge
everything I'd missed. It was the fucking worst, and my
mouth always smelled like old food. Not to mention I
was so determined to suck my thumb at night that I just
ended up shoving it into my skull to make room. The
dentist removed it a month after it had been installed.
My mom's hopes of slapping braces on me and straight-
ening this crooked smile were dashed in an instant. I
sucked my thumb the entirety of the car ride home in
celebration.

Twenty-plus years later and I'm still sitting awake watching new lovers fall asleep so that I don't have to explain my
filthy habit to them. Or, worse than that, entertain questions
like "Why don't you just stop?" or "Have you considered hyp-

nosis?" If this book makes any money, maybe I'll go to therapy and figure out why this grown-ass woman still carries around a baby blanket. Until then, I'm sucking on my therapy. Man, that's so fucking gross. I didn't mean it like that. Ugh. God. Barf.

*i should have a car
with power windows by now*

Today, February 13, 2013, is my birthday. I am excited because I am thirty-three years old and the idea of a man in my life totally bores me. I don't have a college degree. I don't know how to make coffee in a French press. The filter in my humidifier needed to be changed three weeks ago. I should've called the DIRECTV repair person yesterday because my satellite has been out for almost a month but I've been too busy to fucking notice. I'm hoping this triple-chocolate brownie I'm eating doesn't have as many calories as I think it does. My sinuses are killing me. I cried at a commercial for canned cat food. I love drinking LaCroix even though it is more expensive than I can justify. I hate using skid-resistant paper clips. I can't decide how many pairs of yoga pants crosses the apathy line. I hate closed-toed shoes. I can't keep a schedule. I can't remember shit I agree to do, thus rendering every social engagement the worst kind of surprise. I don't like beets no matter how much you people keep foisting them on me.

I never check my e-mail. My home phone has 4,627 unanswered messages on it and I can't remember the password. I still buy fish sticks, the kid kind. I like yogurt because I hate chewing. I feel like listening to *This American Life* every once in a while makes up for the fact that I haven't read a real newspaper since high school. I like to wear maxi pads even when I'm not on my period, because leakage. I have been in love exactly seven times and I want that feeling again before I fucking die. Sometimes I like ginger; sometimes I hate ginger. Food labels confuse me, and serving sizes come from hell. No, really, if I could eat a one-fourth cup of something and walk away from it that would be a miracle. I keep adding books to my Kindle before I've finished reading the books already on it and that intimidates me but it's my own fault. Chelsea Handler's books make me laugh, hard. I love Paul Mooney, even though he sometimes makes me feel like I'm not black enough. I've given up on Sudoku. *Words with Friends* is my shit, but I feel guilty when I beat people. This iPhone is the greatest thing I've ever owned.

I need to stop opting for paperless billing because I never remember to check when my utilities are due, and so my shit is always just about to get shut off. I need to take it easy on myself. I need to get the Internet at home. I need to add more potassium to my diet. I need to be on a motherfucking diet. I need to go swimming. I need a ticket to California. I need a back rub. I need some orthotics in my stupid shoes. I need new sheets. I need a pedicure. I need to be more compassionate. I need to put this taco down and go for a goddamned walk. I need to stop buying cutesy shit at Paper Source that I will never use. I need to not order both a side of sausage and a side of potatoes when eating an already loaded brunch plate. I need to know more about wine regions. I need to do a better job cleaning my ears. I need to take my glasses off before I fall asleep at night. I need to buy baking soda. I need to keep a calendar. I need to pick one when I go out: EATING THINGS or DRINKING THINGS because doing both makes me poor. I need to consolidate my bank shit. I need some clogs. I need a windfall. I need to get some Tiger Balm at the pharmacy. I need this phone to stop ringing. I need this estrogen beard to slow the fuck down. I need salsa and chips, like, every day. I need to visit my niece twins in Michigan because they are getting SO BIG and I am basically missing all of it; they are a year old now and pretty soon will be driving and I will be *that* person and my heart will be broken. I need a goddamned website. I need some sedatives. I need to finish this book. I need to moisturize my cuticles.

I want a baby panda. I want all my Spotify mixes to be the goddamned jam. I want to have a better understanding of world politics. I want Res to make another album. I want a closet full of maxi dresses. I also want a durable chafe cream that won't make wearing those dresses pure fucking torture. I want a Batmobile. I want Christian Bale to drive me around in it while Bane and I make out in the backseat. I want a slow cooker. I want a lifetime supply of C.O. Bigelow frankincense candles. I want to spend an entire weekend in bed watching *Grey's Anatomy* on Netflix. I want some fancy skin cream. I want a tooth implant. I want to be able to dance like Beyoncé. I want some peace and quiet. I want my mama. I want my blankie. I want fresh flowers. I want the cat to lose three pounds so I can stop feeling so guilty. I want my life to be exactly like the movie *Love Jones*. I want Larenz Tate. I want an artsy dude who is sexy and likes my jokes.

I want to hear someone who means it tell me how much he loves me. I want that one guy to pay as much attention to me as I have been paying to him. I want to get off Facebook. I want my fauxhawk to look perfect all the time. I want to get a cleaning lady. I want to cook a squash without fucking it up. I want underwear that comes up to my chin, every single day.

I should have a car with power windows by now. I should live in an apartment that has central air-conditioning. I should get my hair cut. I should take more multivitamins. I should get a new bed. I should bleach the tub. I should read more Toni Morrison novels. I should stop buying so many age-inappropriate magazines. I should have a budget. I should eat more fiber. I should get decent pillows. I should reopen my Match.com and actually take it seriously this time. I should listen to my voice mail. I should sleep with those hand braces I bought a year ago. I should get an ergonomic desk chair. I should scrape the burnt shit out of the inside of the oven. I should scoop the cat box. I should return the cable box I haven't used in three years. I should stop sucking my thumb. I should stop buying liquid hand soap three at a time because even though it's on sale I am only one person and can only wash my hands *so many goddamned times.* I shouldn't buy so much ice cream. I should volunteer more. I should buy some more fancy J.Jill pants in case I get invited someplace T-shirts and flip-flops and hoodies are unacceptable.

I still have two VHS tapes. My apartment has only one chair. My dish towels match, but one is faded due to an accidental bleaching and that bothers me. I have to figure out what to do with my dad's ashes because they've been in a box in my hall closet for years and that just isn't nice. I wish I had the entire *The Fresh Prince of Bel-Air* series on DVD. I would watch it every day. I'm really good at *Family Feud*. I hate the feel of carpet on my bare feet. The beach totally grosses me out. I really love Tom Cruise, seriously more than any other celebrity person. I would like to meet Tom Cruise, and hug him. I need a winning lottery ticket.

ooh, dessert.
and cocktails!

· ·

When I was a junior in high school I used to babysit a whole bunch of kids who lived in this supernice neighborhood in northwest Evanston. This was a giant network of families. I think my dad was a limo driver for one of them and I started taking care of one woman's baby on Saturday nights, nervously perched on the edge of the couch watching *Renegade* and *Walker, Texas Ranger* while hoping that the baby stayed asleep in her crib until her parents rolled in reeking of pinot grigio. I'm not convinced that I did a good job, but for whatever reason the mom kept asking me back to leave trails of Goldfish crumbs scattered across her plush sofa and try to watch rented Blockbuster videos on her complicated TV-VCR set up. I have no idea what she paid me, but I do remember that at the time it felt like a million dollars.

I babysat for her entire circle of friends, skittish and apologetic every time I turned up on the doorstep of a $1 million–plus Victorian with Smashing Pumpkins blaring out of my headphones. I spent hours and hours chasing toddlers who were dressed nicer than I was through cavernous rooms filled with the kind of toys that kids can, like, get into. When I was a kid I had a footstool that Mom copped at a yard sale and I wrote my name on it with nail polish and referred to it as my "special chair"; Hunter had a playroom next to his real room that had a miniature replica spaceship he could lock himself into when he objected to going down for a nap. Once, when I got to their house early, Hunter's mom ("I'm like a cool mom, Sam. Want some weed?") was hanging out in the kitchen and she asked if I wanted some ice cream. Well, duh, I never don't want ice cream. And then she did the most shocking thing I had ever seen in my young, dumb life: she pulled out an ice cream scoop, then she pulled out a pint of New York Super Fudge Chunk, and she scooped perfectly rounded little mounds of ice cream into a bowl.

I wasn't raised behind a garage. I'd seen a spoon and a bowl before, but never had I ever seen an adult-type human not eat directly from a pint of precious ice cream. When I saw her yank open the "not the forks but also not the Chinese menus" drawer and pull out the scooper, I assumed this was some sort of gallon situation and braced myself for her to remove a tub the size of a Toyota out of the industrial freezer full of Pedialyte freezer pops and bagged ravioli. What in the self-soothing emotional hell is this? I thought pints were supposed to be single fucking servings?!

So typically, especially on a weeknight, my dessert-making skills are as follows:

Step 1: Procure pint of Ben & Jerry's Mint Chocolate Cookie ice cream.

Step 2: Leave said ice cream on counter for several minutes to soften while keening impatiently.

Step 3: Eat ice cream a quarter of the way down, vow to stop.

Step 4: Contemplate returning ice cream to freezer.

Step 5: Swear not to consume more than half this ice cream tonight.

Step 6: Okay, but if I don't finish it all that's still a win, right?

Step 7: (Buries empty carton under various trash in wastebasket, head hung in shame.)

Sometimes when I'm somehow feeling both better and worse about myself, I'll order some tubes of cookie dough with my grocery delivery (order: economy-size package of paper towels, some variation of lettuce that hopefully won't spoil before I figure out what to do with it, a roll of Nestlé Toll House, whatever snack cracker sounds vaguely healthy) and bake it with an apron on so that I feel like I'm actually working and making something, i.e., doing something that is worthy of the reward of freshly baked cookies. And, if I'm feeling particularly fancy, I'll sprinkle a little flaked sea salt over the misshapen mounds of dough shining wetly on the one cookie sheet I keep forgetting to buy protective foil for.

And it's fine to eat dry children's cereal over the trash can while scrolling through your ex-girlfriend's timeline at two in the morning, or to make a pot of coffee for the specific purpose of dunking Little Debbie Donut Sticks in it, but what are you gonna do when it's time for book club and you've been tasked with bringing a dessert and you don't want to further embarrass yourself by rolling through with a box of (already open) Famous Amos when you already know you have to fake like you actually read and understood the book? So make something easy and maybe Vanessa won't give you a hard time for quitting after chapter three.

SPICY FLOURLESS CHOCOLATE CAKE

You need

>   7 tablespoons unsalted butter, cut up
>   10 ounces semisweet chocolate chips
>   5 large eggs, room temperature
>   1 cup sugar
>   ½ teaspoon cinnamon
>   ¾ teaspoon ancho chili powder
>   ⅛ teaspoon cayenne pepper
>   pinch of salt

1. Preheat the oven to 350 degrees Fahrenheit. Line the bottom of a 9½-inch springform pan with a circle of parchment paper. Okay, I understand if at this point you're like "Welp, fuck this difficult shit!" But I promise

you that if this was hard I would never do it. I got my first pan at a hardware store. I mean, this is not an intimidating thing. You can get parchment paper at Target or the grocery store and then watch a three-minute You-Tube video if you don't know how to line it. Don't be scared. Once you're done with all that and feeling super smart and accomplished and capable, coat the sides and the parchment with nonstick cooking spray because the physical act of greasing a pan is revolting.

2. I'm sure there's a case to be made for using the double-boiler method to melt chocolate but I'm not gonna be the one to do it. Melt the chocolate and butter together in a microwave at 50 percent power, stirring every couple of minutes, until it's smooth.

3. Whisk the eggs and the sugar together, then slowly add in the melted chocolate a little bit at a time. Once it's all incorporated, add in the spices and whisk for another minute. Some people might test the batter at this stage to make sure the spices are to their liking, but I once missed two weeks of school due to an undercooked pumpkin muffin, so I don't fuck with uncooked eggs. Unprotected sex with a virtual stranger? Sure, why not! A drop of raw yolk landing someplace on my actual skin? SET MY ENTIRE BODY ON FIRE.

4. Pour the batter into the springform pan, scraping down the sides of the bowl to get it all out, then bake for twenty-five minutes (plus or minus), or until a toothpick comes out clean. The idea of toothpicks grosses

me out, so I usually use a strand of dry spaghetti (a spa-ghetto?) to serve this purpose. Which means I *usually* eyeball it and try to inconspicuously poke at the center to make sure it's firm and that I'm not going to poison any innocent women who just showed up armed with homemade artichoke dip and red zinfandel to argue over *NW* or *Gone Girl*.

5. Let it cool on a rack and then unclip the pan to release your chocolate prize. You can serve it plain, but some-times I like to, you know, subtly let people know how much better than them I am, so I like to get out my little mesh strainer and press some powdered sugar through it to decorate the top. This is wholly unnecessary, as no one would ever suspect me of being any kind of chef, but it does look very pretty on a plate.

THINGS THAT ARE DECIDEDLY NOT DESSERT

cheese
grilled fruit
a handful of trail mix
a rice cake with applesauce on it
peanut butter
zucchini bread (I mean, it says "bread" right in the name)
a mashed frozen banana
port (just YUCK, OMG)

· · · · ·

My favorite cocktail of all time is "lukewarm beer guzzled directly over the sink," but that's not where I'm always trying to be in my life. I know that drinking alone is supposed to be sad, but isn't it just as fucking sad to drink in front of people, especially when they are *probably* judging you and it *definitely* costs more to do so? After the first drink, the "let me pretend I don't want every single one of these appetizers" drink, I'm pretty good. I've made it to the restaurant; my shoes haven't yet become totally unbearable; my underwire hasn't begun painfully digging into the not-armpit-yet-not-actually-breast meat on my left side; no cheese grease dripped down the front of my shirt; no one's irritated the poor server with their annoying preferences or dietary restrictions; life is grand! And I'm probably going to order a gin cocktail to start things off, especially if it's one I can't make at home because let's be for real: I AM NOT SPENDING REAL MONEY ON VERMOUTH.

THE CLASSIC NEGRONI

Ingredients
   1 part gin
   1 part Campari
   1 part vermouth

I started drinking Campari when I was young because I would hang out at the studio with Mel all the time, and he liked to pretend he was Italian and stopped work at 3:00 p.m. every day to drink Campari and soda while reading the news and yell at Cubs games on TV. Campari is totally disgusting, but it's disgusting in the same way that all other things are disgusting. Coffee tastes like dirt a car drove through, wine tastes like spoiled grapes someone left out in the sun, and beer tastes like a baby diaper after you accidentally fed it too much bread. It's a means to an end, right? So you suffer through the torturous part (the first time I had Jameson I was in a room with a bunch of ~cool poets~ and I didn't want them to know that I'm the kind of person who enjoys piña coladas unironically so I accepted the glass, then took baby sips with tears in my eyes until the room cleared and I could pour it down the sink while dying of shame). And you keep suffering until you numb yourself into finding it enjoyable and then you wake up one day like "Wow, this battery acid is delicious to me." The things we love always hurt us the most, or something like that.

After the first drink I'm feeling warm and brave enough to admit that, yes, I actually came to this place that serves food to eat it. I'm getting whatever bite-size thing they will inevitably serve an odd number of (boy, do I love the awkward "Who gets to eat the last shrimp puff?" mating dance!) and I'm getting drink number two, so I can keep the party going. Although this time it has to be something with bubbles, because I am a monster who likes to pair food with carbon dioxide. So I will have:

THE FRENCH 75

Ingredients

2 ounces gin

¾ ounce fresh lemon juice

¾ ounce simple syrup

2 ounces champagne
twist of lemon
a club soda extra ice with lime

It's near the end of the second drink that I start to rethink my choices to (1) leave the house, and (2) order $14 drinks and consume them out in the world in front of other people. This is the point where my brain signals "Don't have another drink!" at the same time my mouth is forming the words "Yep, I'll have another!" if for no other reason than because my hands need something to occupy them during the twenty minutes it takes for the sous chef to arrange microgreens atop my roast chicken with a pair of tweezers. I'm trying to maintain a two-to-one water-to-cocktail sip ratio but by the time the shiny entrée plate is set in front of me—whoops, whaddya know, this champagne flute is empty again! Now is the time for some reckoning, but I only have three seconds to decide whether to go for number four and yeah I probably shouldn't but Melissa is thumbing through the cocktail list and Emily is blathering on about wines and isn't the reason you waited five weeks for a reservation to this hipster shithole in the first place because you read an article about the mixologist?! That settles it, I'm having one more.

THE SAZERAC

Ingredients
   1 sugar cube
   2½ ounces rye whiskey
   2 dashes Peychaud's bitters
   1 dash Angostura bitters

absinthe
lemon peel
highball glass

I started drinking Sazeracs mostly because the name sounds cool and they taste kind of like medicine, which is comforting to me. I don't have a dog in the whiskey fight, so I don't care what kind the bartender uses, and I'm not sophisticated enough to know the difference anyway. What I *do* know is that I'm never going to be the type of person who stocks multiple types of bitters in her home, so this is the kind of thing I definitely go out for. What I can do: uncork a bottle of Costco wine and pour it into one of the IKEA juice glasses from the cabinet over my sink. What I cannot do: buy absinthe, not break expensive highball glasses, attractively peel a lemon to garnish a drink.

As soon as the dinner plates get cleared I feel like I might throw up. It's a combination of being kinda wasted, staying awake past 9:00 p.m., and making a bunch of terrible food choices because who knows when the goddess of scheduling/finances/ outfits will allow a dinner like this to ever take place again. I'm definitely slurring my words a little bit and there's a pork belly stain on my pants and I would have been happy to leave twenty minutes ago but now we're at the "do we or do we not want to admit this night is over" impasse, when we will clumsily hem and haw over whether it's time for the check and what, if anything, we plan to do once it's paid. This is when I mentally tabulate how unfair each of our shares is and whether I have enough money to take a cab home. I dread the moment that one asshole (usually the youngest of the group but not always) is like, "Sure! I'd love to see the digestifs!" Come on, Jessie. I'm not drinking ouzo while picking at a cheese plate. I have approximately forty minutes to make it to my apartment before I shit in these Spanx and fall asleep in the bathtub. Don't do this to me. But what the hell, the liquor store under the el train around the corner from my apartment where I buy High Life tallboys doesn't sell amaro so sure I'll take two.

When left to my own devices I like to drink pink shit like punches and mai tais. I like to sit in my nice chair with a glass of ice I can regularly ladle punch over until my vision gets too blurry to text and I can roll that chair over to my bed and take a nap. I love a fruity drink, especially when I'm feeling festive and need to celebrate, like when there's a *Real Housewives of New York City* marathon on or one of my friends is in a bad mood and wants to lie around feeling hopeless and casting spells on our mutual enemies. Nothing says "screaming hell demon" like making something called Bad Girl Punch you read about in *Cosmo* that's been seasoned with your own tears.

BAD GIRL PUNCH

Ingredients
- 1 bottle of tequila
- 6 ounces Aperol (I know this seems like a waste of money, but you can mix the rest with wine)
- 4 ounces mescal
- 15 ounces grapefruit juice
- 4 limes
- 6 ounces simple syrup
- 3 pinches sea salt

2 bottles of ginger ale

grapefruit slices for garnish (BUT Y THO)

Mix everything together in a punch bowl, then drink. And I feel you, I DON'T HAVE A PUNCH BOWL, EITHER. But I *do* have a set of those nesting mixing bowls, so what I like to do is wash it really well, to make sure all the cookie dough crumbs and dried cereal milk is out of it, and let it double as a vessel for the booze. I mean, if it's just you, do you care?

I grew up in church, despite all evidence to the contrary, and one of the best things about it was drinking some combination of sherbet and 7UP in the basement after service while sneaking around trying to avoid the pinching fingers of the deaconesses who wanted to catch me bursting out of my scratchy formal dress to tell me how fat I was getting. I drank so many waxy cups of slimy orange drink while hiding in the handicapped stall waiting for my grandmother to count the offering and put away communion so we could go home. Nowadays I prefer this boozy version.

BOOZY SHERBET PUNCH

Ingredients

    1 gallon strawberry sherbet

    1 pint strawberries, hulled and frozen

    12 ice cubes

    2 pints vodka

1 liter ginger ale

1 large can of Hawaiian Punch (drink of the gods)

Scoop the sherbet into a bowl; add strawberries and ice. Pour in vodka, ginger ale, and Hawaiian Punch. Gleefully watch the scoops of sherbet rise to the surface and scheme on how to get more sherbet in your cup than the pastor's daughter gets in hers. Immediately burn with shame at this very un-Jesus-like behavior. Elbow her out of the way anyway, and grab a handful of imitation Nilla wafers, too.

The best thing about punch, other than the consumption of it, is that you don't have to do a lot of precious zesting and shaking; you just throw everything in a bowl and give it a good stir and then you're done. And don't feel shackled to the idea that you can't make punch unless it's a party. Make punch just because it's Tuesday, like this rum punch adapted from the homie Martha Stewart.

TUESDAY RUM PUNCH

Ingredients

1½ cups light rum (or dark—it's your world, do what you want)

3 cups orange juice (she calls for fresh squeezed but, like, LOLWAT)

3 cups pineapple juice (if you juice a pineapple yourself, never talk to me again)

    3 tablespoons fresh lime juice (this I can do)

    2 tablespoons cranberry juice (save the rest for your next
       UTI)

    2 tablespoons grenadine

Combine everything in a large pitcher and stir well to blend. Spray some tropical Febreze on those pajamas you've been wearing for a week and pretend you're on an island somewhere. Serve in red Solo cups over ice, which is how I preferred to drink it that summer I spent a week in Antigua having sex with a hotel porter who actually believed that a twenty-one-year-old person with two roommates and a prepaid cell phone could marry him and better his life in America.

ACKNOWLEDGMENTS

Listen, I only started writing a blog in the halcyon days of 2007
to impress this dude I met on fucking MySpace, because I liked
him and he said he was into writers and I wanted to prove that
I was one but didn't want to give him one hundred out-of-
context pages of the YA novel I was halfheartedly trying to
write. So I started my blog and it was pretty funny, and we had
the kind of relationship that is fraught with stupidity, and when
it ended, I was like "LOL, FUCK THIS BLOG." Plus everyone
had jumped ship and gone to Facebook anyway, so what was
even the point? Laura Munroe and I went out for cheeseburgers and beers at the Morseland one night after work, and she
said, "You should make a real blog!" Fueled by alcohol and a
burning desire to see who else I could lure into bed with my
gross oversharing and awkward self-deprecating jokes, I went
back to my tiny apartment and googled "do people read blogs"
and— Just kidding. I went on blogspot like a normal person
and made a thing I thought no one else was ever gonna see.
Anyway, this wouldn't be a book without my dear Laura, whom
I have tortured with every bad date and limited-edition-snack
request for the better part of a decade, so much so that she

demanded I dump all my bullshit on the internet rather than at her feet. I love you very much. Thank you for making me do this.

My fiercest champions, from my first awkward journal poem about some unrequited crush to this collection of essays about my butt, have always been Anna Galland and Lara Crock. They are two of the smartest, kindest, and most compassionate people I have ever met, and I'm so lucky that they've been my friends for almost my entire life, even though it's totally wild to look someone in the face who remembers what you wore in gym class in 1991. I still cannot believe they have mortgages and children—hell, Lara is a doctor!!—while I could not point out Montana on a map.

I would like to thank all my sisters for never fronting on me in public or airing our collective history. I'm also the proudest aunt of the greatest kids, even though they're all like thirty years old now and have better credit than I do. I mean, Alexis owned a brand-new car while I was still taking the bus. WTF kind of role model even am I?! Ash and Alexis and Travis, I hope you guys are proud.

My heart, forever, belongs to Caitlin Pinsof. Thank you to Carl Cowan, for keeping me sane, every single day. Cara Brigandi and Ted Beranis took me in, like a sad dog left out to shiver in the cold rain, and made a home for me both in their house and in their hearts. I wrote almost the entirety of the first version of this book in their guest room, with the air conditioner turned all the way up, drinking Diet Cokes and bourbon. Megan Stielstra helped shape these essays when they were just blobs of words lumped together and turn them into something cool. Marina and Brad Hayes have taken care of me and adopted me into their LA family. I couldn't have made it through the last two years without them. And much love always to my large adult son, Jessie Mae Martinson.

I can't find my original thank-you list and let's be honest: A LOT OF THOSE PEOPLE DON'T TALK TO ME ANYMORE. But whatever, man, their loss. Anyway, here is a laundry list of people I would like to thank for their love and friendship and inspiration when I was first working on this book and a couple more who helped out the second time around: Brooke Allen, Senam Amegashie, Emily Barish, Ian Belknap, Julia Borcherts, Harold Branch, Ruth Curry, Laura Daener, Isis Ferguson, Kristen Fiore, Melissa Fisher, Angie Frank, Kevin Garvey, Roxane Gay, Julia Goldberg, Emily Gould, Stephani Gray, Chandra Hartman, Jen Hiltwein, Mariyam Hussain, Abbi Jacobson, Keely Jones, Jessi Klein, Katy Maher, Allen Makere, Keila Miranda, Beth Newsome, Carly Oishi, Giancarlo Olvera, Fred Owens, Kate Packard, Nikki Patin, Robyn Pennacchia, Christopher Piatt, Vanessa Robinson, Rainbow Rowell, Akilah Scott, Nina Silguero, John Sundholm, Chris Terry, Dennis Turan, Elissa Wald, Crystal Wells, Lindy West, Sarah Westwood, Claire Zulkey, and all of the OGs. Thank the lord for Janeane Garofalo! And I will be forever grateful that Kirsten Jennings found this book and then found me.

I love every single person at Vintage like they're my children, but I gotta thank Andrea Robinson, Joan Wong, Angie Venezia, and my extremely kind and patient editor, Maria Goldverg, the loudest for making all the moving parts of this process so great. Jason Richman (and Sam Reynolds!) at UTA make being in Hollywood slightly less terrifying. Many thanks to Molly Friedrich and Lucy Carson at The Friedrich Agency. Kent D. Wolf is the smartest, handsomest, funniest, and meanest person I have ever met and also the most perfect human being to ever exist.

Without his friendship and guidance I would be writing my dumb jokes on napkins at the bar and awkwardly testing them out on people peeing in the bathroom. For free.

And finally, Dr. Manoj Mehta made having an embarrassing and unpredictable butt disease almost tolerable, and my life as I know it would not be possible without the kindness, generosity, and support of both my fake dad, Mel Winer, and my real dad, James Hagedorn. Thank you for everything, you turds.